b1119299n

3 9047 00011344 5

APR -7 1997

MAR 11 1993

818
B   BISSELL, RICHARD
              MY LIFE ON THE
           MISSISSIPPI

                                    COPY 2

SAN MATEO PUBLIC LIBRARY,
SAN MATEO, CALIF

D1165744

MY LIFE ON THE MISSISSIPPI

or

WHY I AM NOT MARK TWAIN

MY LIFE
ON THE MISSISSIPPI

or

WHY I AM NOT MARK TWAIN

by RICHARD BISSELL

LITTLE, BROWN AND COMPANY
BOSTON–TORONTO

SAN MATEO PUBLIC LIBRARY, SAN MATEO, CALIFORNIA

COPYRIGHT © 1973 BY RICHARD BISSELL

ALL RIGHTS RESERVED. NO PART OF THIS BOOK MAY BE REPRODUCED
IN ANY FORM OR BY ANY ELECTRONIC OR MECHANICAL MEANS IN-
CLUDING INFORMATION STORAGE AND RETRIEVAL SYSTEMS WITHOUT
PERMISSION IN WRITING FROM THE PUBLISHER, EXCEPT BY A REVIEWER
WHO MAY QUOTE BRIEF PASSAGES IN A REVIEW.

FIRST EDITION

T 11/73

Selections from *A Stretch on the River* by Richard Bissell are reprinted by permission of the author. Copyright 1950 by Richard P. Bissell. Published by Little, Brown and Company in association with The Atlantic Monthly Press.

Library of Congress Cataloging in Publication Data

Bissell, Richard Pike.
    My life on the Mississippi.

    Bibliography: p.
    1. Bissell, Richard Pike. 2. Mississippi River.
3. Clemens, Samuel Langhorne, 1835-1910. I. Title.
F354.B63   917.7'03'30924 [B]   73-14537
ISBN 0-316-096741

*Published simultaneously in Canada
by Little, Brown & Company (Canada) Limited*

PRINTED IN THE UNITED STATES OF AMERICA

COPY 2

To my daughter
Anastasia

Contents

CHAPTER ONE

CHAPTER TWO

CHAPTER THREE

CHAPTER FOUR

CHAPTER FIVE

CHAPTER SIX

CHAPTER SEVEN

CHAPTER EIGHT

CHAPTER NINE

CHAPTER TEN

CHAPTER ELEVEN

CHAPTER SIXTEEN

CHAPTER SEVENTEEN

CHAPTER EIGHTEEN

CHAPTER NINETEEN

CHAPTER TWENTY

APPENDIX

Illustrations

(between pages 174 and 175)

MY LIFE ON THE MISSISSIPPI
or
WHY I AM NOT MARK TWAIN

ONE

"Banned in Dubuque"

T heodore Roosevelt is substantially and to all effects and purposes, insane, and ought to be in an asylum."

Who said that?

Well it wasn't my old man, it was America's Sweetheart, lovable, funny old Mark Twain.

Mark Twain was a nut.

He had small delicate hands, with which he kept a life-time Shit List of people he didn't like. Once you were on that list you never got off. And he did not forget his dead enemies; their deaths represented further impudence. The deader they got the madder he got.

The doctors wouldn't let him into the room to see his wife Livy when she was sick. They figured rightly that laying eyes on him would give her a relapse. When they lived in Riverdale in 1902 the doctors wouldn't let him in to see her for over five months.

He used to wait on Sundays in the lobby of the Plaza Hotel in New York until church was out, then walk down Fifth Avenue in his white suit so everybody coming from church would gawp at him.

His hatreds and "personal vendettas" were sometimes so

persistent and intense that his wife said "you seem almost like a monomaniac."*

William Dean Howells said that Livy was *glad* to be sick and confined to her room in order to get away from the constant repetitive bickering and hollering about "the damned human race."

Samuel Langhorne Clemens, Mark Twain, was born in Florida, Missouri, in 1835. Died Redding, Connecticut, 1910.

Unfortunately he wagged his head from side to side when he walked, a peculiarly unattractive trait bringing to mind somehow Franklin Roosevelt, Jimmy Cagney, and Felix the Cat.

His faithful and true lifelong friend Howells said that Clemens smiled at you with "remote absence." I know it well. That's my cousin Archie. "You were all there for him, but he was not all there for you." Actually it doesn't bother me to see that scrim come down between Archie and me. But some people find it very trying.

Mark Twain never went to the theatre. You know why, don't you? Just like my cousin Archie — hates the theatre, won't go, says it's a fraud, tickets too high. That's not the reason, the reason is, there are people up there on the stage talking and talking and talking and he never gets a chance to talk. Can't say a word. This is the most unendurable torture to a natural born wind artist and compulsive interrupter; he has got to blow every so often, like a whale, or die right in the fourth row.

America's favorite chucklesome after-dinner speaker loathed banquets, was in mortal agony listening to the other speeches, and finally worked out a system where he sneaked

---

* Justin Kaplan (*Mr. Clemens and Mark Twain*), like The Shadow, sees all, knows all.

in after the guzzling and preliminaries, gave his talk, and faded out again into the street.

Because I myself write books about the Mississippi River, because I used to be a pilot on the Mississippi River and hold a pilot's license on the Mississippi River today, the critics for twenty-three years have been calling me "a modern Mark Twain." Now is this fair?

I wasn't born in a little frame shanty down in Missouri, wouldn't think of it. I was born in splendor at the top of the Fourth Street elevator in Dubuque, Iowa, Key City to the West, greatest state in the Union. Missouri — no thanks!

When *my* wife is sick the doctors don't send me down to the Elks Club.

I don't wag my head when I walk and I don't have small, delicate hands, either. Beautiful, strong, capable artistic hands, maybe.

The way it happened was, after I gave up steamboating on the Mississippi, the Ohio, the Tennessee, the Cumberland, the St. Croix, the Kanawha, the Tygart and the Monongahela I wrote a novel* ("picaresque," brother Mycroft said and he began to talk about Cervantes) about towboating on the Upper Mississippi. It was published in Boston by William Dean Howells' old outfit, so I was in good company there.

Everybody was surprised, especially the folks on Arlington Street in Boston, when the book started getting "hailed." It was hailed in the New York papers and it was hailed in Boston, Providence, Fall River, and Worcester, as well as down in Philadelphia and clear across the continent to the Sacramento Valley. It was one of the biggest hailstorms on record and it was a straight case of ". . . not since Mark Twain . . ." ". . . in the tradition of Mark Twain . . ."

---

* *A Stretch on the River* (Boston, Atlantic, 1950).

My luck being what it is, the publishers had expected to sell only about 23 copies, so when the hailing hit, most of the bookstores were without any stock. I have since learned that even if a book, any book, sells 100,000 copies, the book stores still don't have any stock. Or sometimes they have some copies but they are in with the law books by mistake.

Anyway the Chicago *Trib* said ". . . roughest, rawest . . . Mark Twain . . ." And the Philadelphia *Bulletin*'s Mr. Bernard Bergman said ". . . takes its place with Mark Twain . . . poetry . . ." St. Louis *Post Dispatch:* ". . . lusty, bawdy . . . virile . . . poetry . . . women . . . fun . . ." *Time* said ". . . Mark Twain . . ."

In Dubuque my book was simultaneously hailed by the newspaper and banned by the Catholic Mothers Purity Association. They even had a hearing on it during which Paul Engle, poet laureate of Iowa, testified in my defense. That sets me into a more popular category than Mark Twain right away. Was he ever banned in Hannibal? Getting your books banned in Boston used to be easy enough, but get these headlines: MODERN MARK TWAIN BANNED IN DUBUQUE!!

Times have changed. Last year a Dubuque lad published a book about growing up in the parochial schools there that I wouldn't lend to a lascar coal passer, but no word has been heard from the Catholic Mothers. A lot has happened in 23 years. Most of it unfortunate.

So that's how it is that when I stop at the store in Beetown, Wisconsin, to get two bottles of Dubuque Star beer and a box of Uneedas, the store lady says, "Say — I seen you someplace in the paper already. Ain't you that modern Mark Twain from over at Dubuque?" And I have to admit I am.

And it explains why I am besieged for "Modern Mark

Twain" autographs whenever I stroll down Michigan Boulevard, Powell Street, or Fifth Avenue.

But I don't think I am really much like Mark Twain. Maybe I write better, but listen, folks, he came from Missouri and for a chalk-talk man he did all right. I just had the advantages is all. He would of been the first to admit it.

And I've got some pretty nice tattoos, also. If Mark Twain had had any tattoos don't you just think he would have talked them up? You know it. And Albert Bigelow Paine, when he wrote the authorized and studgy biography, don't you know if his subject had had glorious cutaneous stars, eagles, tigers, and anchors like I have, how he would have bragged them up? Kaplan* knows more about Mark Twain than anybody and he never says a word about tattoos.

If we are going to be geniuses together, it is all right with me. But it's not just roses all the way. He had his ups and downs the same as I have had and not everybody thought he was such hot stuff.

In a standard late nineteenth century work called *American Literature*, one Professor Charles F. Richardson does not mention Mark Twain under fiction at all, and gives him three lines under humor, saying "temporary amusement, not literary product, is the thing sought and given." That's enough out of you, Richardson. But he was not alone.

"Grandma," I asked my grandmother Bissell one wintry afternoon in the 1920's, high on the hill over the Mississippi in Dubuque. "If Mark Twain is one of our greatest American writers, why does he sometimes say 'he don't' and 'she don't' instead of 'he doesn't' and 'she doesn't'?"

"Because he didn't know any better," she said.

"He was very common, you might say trashy," she added.

"But Grandma, at school Miss Sheridan says . . ."

* Kaplan.

"Hark!" she said. "What's that noise?" All the Bissells were great at shouting "Hark!"

"They're just putting coal in Mrs. Burch's coal chute," I said.

"Mark Twain! Good heavens what are we coming to?"

"But Miss Sheridan at school says he was a genius. 'Genius in its purest form' she says."

"Genius fiddlesticks! Sitting around there in Hartford drinking whiskey with his cronies and smoking cigars — forty cigars a day — tell your Miss Sheridan that. As far as I can see he never dined alone with his family, *always* had *some*body to prance and spout in front of, that ruffian Bret Harte, or some illiterate steamboat pilot or such, anybody would do him. I declare if it came dinnertime and nobody there but his wife and the girls, I'll wager he went out in the street and collared the first three or four people he met. And then, every single meal so they say, while everybody is eating, *he's* up from the table maundering up and down jawing a mile a minute. Can you imagine Mr. Holmes or Mr. Hawthorne showing such disgraceful manners?

"Here's your genius for you. At one of these dinners Mark Twain and a gentleman from the neighborhood decided to write a book together, on a bet with their wives. Richard, geniuses do not collaborate. Can you imagine Charles Dickens getting full of wine and deciding to collaborate on a book with some man from across the street?"

"Well, no I can't, I guess," I said. "Who was the man?"

"Charles Dudley Warner, and the book, which was outrageous, was *The Gilded Age*."

"Who was Charles Dudley Warner, Grandma?"

"Oh heavens my dear, a complete nobody. To give you some idea, he was the editor of one of those atrocities called

Treasury of the World's Best Literature or some such title. You can imagine that if you like."

I tried to imagine it but couldn't get very far with it.

"Of course," she said, "he realized later that the book was a very skimpy affair which is putting it mildly, but he never could admit he was wrong about anything, oh certainly not, not the great Mark Twain, so he said it was *Warner*'s fault, that Warner had talked him into it. Oh he was a devious one, a mean one."

"I guess you don't like Mark Twain very much," I said.

"A buffoon," she said. "Here, here's a good book for a boy to read on a nice snowy afternoon," and she gave me my grandfather's copy of *Lavengro* by George Borrow.

But a lot of people felt that way about Mark Twain and a lot of them still do. This doesn't make it any easier for me being "A Modern Mark Twain."

MARK TWAIN IN VENICE

"You enter, and proceed to that most-visited little gallery that exists in the world — the Tribune — and there, against the wall, without obstructing rag or leaf, you may look your fill upon the foulest, the vilest, the obscenest picture the world possesses — Titian's *Venus*."

TWO

Well That's a Poor Attitude

Mark Twain always said he loved piloting and the river, and so did I. As usual *he* laid it on pretty heavy:

"Piloting on the Mississippi River was not work to me; it was play — delightful play, vigorous play, adventurous play — and I loved it."

I got carried away like that myself sometimes. I used to say "Just imagine me getting *paid* to pilot a steamboat! Why it's like getting *paid* to drive a fire engine."

But it wasn't all fun. Despite what he says about a pilot being "the only unfettered and entirely independent human being that lived on the earth," all pilots have always had their bad times like everybody else, even though the pilot is an "absolute monarch who was absolute in sober truth and not by a fiction of words."

When he was a cub pilot, Sam Clemens refused to fill in on the big old *Pennsylvania* and stand a day watch alone, because he was afraid. It's not uncommon. "But I was afraid; I had never stood a watch of any sort by myself, and I believed I should be sure to get into trouble in the head of some chute, or ground the boat in a near cut through some bar or other."

I don't blame him a bit, especially on that nasty Lower Mississippi, which was the only river he knew.*

Pilots had all kinds of troubles, and they still do. They had troubles with boats which steered badly and handled erratically, troubles with the channel, with the weather, wind, floods, low water, troubles with bridges, landings, locks, troubles with the engine room, the galley, the mate, the pilot-house windows which rattled constantly and had to have wooden wedges stuck here and there which soon fell out; troubles with too little heat in the pilot house and too much heat in the pilot house, troubles with the god damn owners, and always troubles with the river itself, for it never stands still.

Here's the kind of thing that can happen when indulging in the "delightful play, adventurous play" of piloting a steam towboat for example (NOTE: The captain who Fraser Mc-Lellan describes here was not only captain but also stood a full pilot's watch. In Mark Twain's day they had two pilots, plus a captain who only managed the boat and kidded the lady passengers — what we call a "roof captain" today):

While captain of the *Sailor*, Hiernaux was troubled and handicapped when first taking over by some of the deckhands walking off the job. The first World War was on and the army had taken most of the young men. "What we had to work with," says Captain Hiernaux, "was older men who had done much drinking. I hardly ever took my clothes off to go to bed. I slept in the

---

* In addition to the pomp and majesty of the piloting profession, he seems to have gloried in the pilot's right, if he cared to use it, of hollering at the crew and bossing around everybody in sight. Years and years later he said, "By long habit, pilots came to put all their wishes in the form of commands. It 'gravels' me, to this day, to put my will in the weak shape of a request, instead of launching it in the crisp language of an order."

Nice guy to have around.

And believe me he meant it all the way down the line.

pilot house. I was to have two deckhands and a watchman which would make three men on watch. Often I would have only one deckhand and a mate and that kept me on watch all the time. Some days I would have a full crew and think I was lucky. I would enter the lock with six barges. I would put four barges in one lock and the towboat and the other two barges in the other lock. It was necessary to have the four barges unfastened from the two barges tied to the knees of the towboat. When it came time to unfasten them, there would not be a deckhand near them. I would look down the lock wall and there would be the deckhands all dressed up and walking away from the boat. So I would have to go and turn the barges loose myself. The pilot would do the piloting while I did the deckhand work.

A captain I worked for once on the Upper Mississippi was a wonderful pilot but he also was pretty high strung. He smoked a pipe and used to chew up about two pipe stems a month. Coming down through the vicious Clinton Pool above Lock 13 with thirteen empty barges in a November snow and wind storm, he bit his pipe stem right in two. That's not fun steamboating up there with empties in the fall of the year. And we never had anything but empties: coal loads up, empties down.

Another pilot had a grand lot of vigorous fun when the rough water in Keokuk Pool got into the engine room and sank the boat, the old *Wheelock Whitney*, formerly the *W. A. Shepard*. The only thing showing was the stacks and the top of the pilot house.

Over on the Ohio River every so often a pilot gets out of shape and goes over one of those crazy dams they have over there. This is glorious sport.

Here's an account of a pilot taking a very small towboat up a river he has never seen before, sometimes at night, on a flood stage of water, with a boat that steered very badly, yawing all over hell.

Note the typical cool composure and casual attitude of this fearless pilot. ("Pilots were like Gods, and like the Gods they were infallible.")

The boat was upbound from Cincinnati on the Ohio River to Brownsville, Pennsylvania, on the Monongahela River.

The pilot, "master of all he surveyed," was me.

February 22, 1944
M/V Brokamp
Pomeroy, Ohio
Mile 249.7

Dearest Medio and Baby Tommy:

Proceeding up O.K. Got through last night O.K. running through maze of bridges, locks, tipples, landings, abandoned piers and sunken vessels. Fog today. Made Gallipolis Lock this afternoon and passed the town — also Point Pleasant and Marietta Mfg. Co. Shower baths on this boat really work. This may be classed as a typical good ole push boat, except for the pilot house engine control which is sheer murder. We ran out of the high water and now into another rise, these river towns are just marvelous. Now passing Syracuse, pop 678, and there are more beautiful old houses than in whole state of W. Va. I am feeling better, a swell evening and I am seated here in the pilot house beside the cozy stove. 14 full windows in pilot house. Inside staircase to officers' quarters and galley. Milk in wax containers. Ham and eggs and peaches only food for 4 days — also bread and oleomarg. and peanut butter. And coffee. Lots of boats down today. Charles T. Campbell appeared out of the fog looming up like the Berengaria *on Turkey River.*

She sure steers hard. Callouses from winding that damn wheel. Another night watch facing me soon. Don't care for them at all on an unfamiliar river. I have persuaded capt. to let me have the deckhand up on night watch instead of days — a big help. River is narrowing down — we're 250 miles from Pittsburgh now. Then 45 miles up to Brownsville. Our bunkroom is great. Plenty windows and built in bunks; a little passageway with shower and head across. Staircase down to galley and up to pilot house. Suppose I will go back to Shamrock *— but what the hell — she handles so much better, that will be nice anyway. Say hello to everybody. Our blankets are brand new and 85% wool — cost 7.50 apiece. Boy they are great — not covered with grease and fuel oil and dirt.*

Love from BISS

Wheeling, W. Va.
Feb. 25, 44
25 days until vac.
(I hope)

Dearest Wife and Babe:
    I have been thinking of you all afternoon as we came up-river struggling against what is now a flood. I haven't anything to say, except I love you both and hope you are happy and Mamma please get our quota of booze honey. It is 7:00 PM and I'll to bed so I can face the situation at midnight well rested. Bad stage of water. I ran into a floating tree last night in the dark. It is folly to run nights in this kind of water with light boat (no barges) but that's Central Barge Co. We should be in Pittsburgh tomorrow night this time if we lose no time tonight. I bought gum drops from a man in a row-boat-type store at Parkersburg. They are only fair. He rows

out to meet all the boats. River still rising. Tonight will be my last night of it on the Ohio I think and hope. This has been a wild ole trip. Glad I am making it in spite of night hazards, no food, and dopy captain.

Lock No. 10
Ohio River
Mile 66.2
Feb. 26, 1944

Dearest Wife:

Well we tied up tonight. Capt. ran until midnight and had a hell of a time with drift and the flood so we decided to lay up. We are tied up to the right bank above Lock 10, Ohio River. I've been sitting here in the pilot house reading Waterways Journal *and old Pittsburgh papers. It's 4 AM now. It's rather a shame but I cannot seem to fix my mind on anything of permanent interest and am only able to keep a sense of being alive by thinking of my responsibilities and satisfaction of being a family man. I have almost given up planning on the future, especially the future with Central Barge Co. No use in wondering whether I'll be on here steady or not, or whether I'll ever get a chance at Marmet, or whether I could get a shore job in Joliet. The old quarterboat from which I have called you so many times, and in whose dusty rooms I have waited for so many boats has burned; Joliet will seem strange without the quarterboat and its big blackboard showing the crews of all the boats and the Coke machine and littered desks.*

I hate being in such a lacklustre condition. When I get rested up and procure some new books from the drugstore in Morgantown I may take some active interest in life again. I guess I am pretty tired out. It seems strange, almost unbeliev-

able and remote — that evening in Van Wert, Ohio, with the heavy snow swirling around the streetlights as I crossed the muffled streets from steak at Balyeats to "Hello Frisco Hello" and then had a strawberry soda in a store that smelled of drugs like Pottervelds. There was almost no one on the streets, and when I came in the hotel the clerk and four traveling salesmen had pulled their chairs into a semicircle around the big window in the lobby and were smoking cigars, watching the storm and laughing quietly at each other. "Boy she's really some night out," I said to the elevator boy. It was one of the best nights I can remember. Another good one was the night you sat in a Galena tavern and I walked through the snow. Another was a night we went to an amusement park with Greeley and had a welsh rarebit and National Premium beer. Then a night at Sherrills Mound when we had a picnic and strawberry cones — that was before everything went to hell.

Time to open a can of peaches. We are almost entirely out of food and Gilliam won't stop to go ashore.

Congo, West Virginia, is twelve miles up the river.

I am starting to brood and dream about food.

"A night without girls is a night wasted." Days also. What a wasted life I'm leading.

Daddy

Monongahela River
Feb. 26, 1944

Dearest Medio:

We're 2 miles below Brownsville and my nerves are shot. Thank heaven we are this far anyway. Last night I had all of Pittsburgh and 12 miles up the Monongahela. You can't imagine the traffic. I didn't know where I was any of the time

and boats coming at me from all directions. Went through
sixteen *bridges.* Finally at 5:20 arrived at a lock, with 4
boats ahead of me waiting to get through so laid against the
bank and that episode was over. Forgot to say visibility was
reduced materially by rain smoke and fog. No more of that
for me. This afternoon I passed 18 boats, all of them steam
sternwheelers, except those belonging to our friend J. Laugh-
lin, which were steam screw propellers. Last night was really
something — I guess you can picture it. This has been some
experience. Heavy drift all the way. Bad at night of course.*

*We'll be in the shipyard soon and will drydock no doubt
tomorrow. Oh what a blessed relief not to have to get up at
midnight and enter the pilot house and peer out into the
pitchy black. I finally got down to a system on night running
— had the deckhand read the lights to me as we proceeded
— got so could run fairly well except fierce drift and steering
very badly. Light book 4 years out of date so of course occasionally would get balled up hunting for a mark which has
been discontinued. I guess Crazy Mike will be transferred
and I'll be working with Gilliam, Ironjaw, or Curley — all
very satisfactory gents. We are entirely out of food. Had
canned corn and Corn Flakes with molasses for supper. God
damn silly. I did get two packages of licorice in Wellsville
yesterday when I went uptown to send grams and letters to
the office and to you. Ate them last night while in hell, and it
helped a lot. One time this afternoon I found myself scram-
bled up in the midst of 6 steam towboats all churning up and
down and all over the place, blowing hundreds of whistles at
each other and me. It's a real education. I've always heard of
"The Pittsburgh Pools" and now I have seen what goes on
with my own eyes. Christ what a spot and river to put a new*

* Note to Capt. Fred Way Jr.: Is this possible, Cap?

pilot. It is to be noted that I coolly sneered my way through All. I feel so much better since I shaved. I smoke too much on watch, from being either nervous or bored. Steel mills all day — hundreds of them! I miss you, darling.

We are all pretty nerved up and ornery. Even the engineers have had lots of trouble. But I'm not complaining. As the feller said, "These are the goddamnedest eggs I ever tasted . . . but I like 'em!"

I am starting to act in regard to pilot's exam. Wrote Ingersoll for document of service on Monongahela, etc. Bought stamped envelopes at Wellsville, Ohio.

Here we are at the marine ways, thank God. Will get pulled out tomorrow. We have an awful lot of repairs but will probably . . .

> *Hillman Barge & Construction Co.*
> *Brownsville Pa.*
> *Monongahela River Mile 56.0*
> *Feb. 27*

Well we're out. Situation was like this:

Port backing rudder had a log jammed in it and was inoperative.

There was a tree jammed in under the starboard backing rudder and continuing on under the propeller shaft. The starboard backing rudder itself was bent all to hell and off the rudder stock.

About thirty feet of wire cable was wrapped around the propeller and shaft.

The driving rudder was crunched and a real pretzel.

How the hell did we get here?

Only superior piloting and superb seamanship obviously, plus NO BRAINS.

When I think of me zooming around in the Pittsburgh Pools with my rudders in this shape it makes my hair stand on end, and considering the length of my hair that is quite a feat. Oboy, we'll be here for several days. Movies. Tavern. Steaks. Beer. Sodas. (Two miles to town, no bus.)

Unless they ship me to Morgantown.

3 letters from you. Paper. Waterways Journal. *2 letters from Dad. One letter from "Pearl Harbor" (former deckhand). The Montgomery Ward catalogue is in Morgantown waiting for me. It will be rather heavy in my suitcase.*

Boats seen yesterday. All steam sternwheelers:

Vulcan	J. H. Hillman
Mac-Rod	Prosperity
Vesta	(diesel sternwheel)
A. O. Ackard	Edgar Thomson
Homestead	Mongah
Crescent	La Belle
Dravo 43 (diesel)	John L. Howder
Wm. Larimer Jones	Pittsburgh Coal
William Whigham	Sailor

It will be O.K. if you're in the hospital with the new baby when I come home on vacation. I'll come and read the paper to myself. You'll probably be out some of the time though. Shipyard is making new rudders. I'm watching them. Riveting noises everywhere. Constant stream of boats going past. Drifting clouds in blue sky. I ain't doing a damn thing but set. 9 hours of dreamless sleep last night. Pounding noises now on stern. I always like being in drydock.

Enclosing towing bonus check for Dec.

The reason pilot-house control is no good is because it sticks, jams, fucks up, and you can't throttle down to a real slow bell at all.

Figures show the heaviest river tonnage in the world *over this stretch from here to Pittsburgh. More tonnage through these locks than thru Panama Canal!*

Wonder how long before capt. is going to try to get me to work while laying here. I have no gloves anyway. He ain't saying nothing but he is giving me those looks. I think I earned a little rest coming up. Capt. now confesses he was scairt to death all the way up. I wasn't, but I had a hell of a night down at Pittsburgh.

Lots of jokes from Trierweiler about my Monkey Ward catalogue. Wrote Winslow Hillman Partridge Wood and Van Huesen for letters to the steamboat inspectors. The prospect of a square meal sometime today is earning some points. Be sure to tell F. E., Sr., what's been going on, and thanks for letters; I'll write soon as I get a chanct.

Maybe I can get a ride into town this evening from a welder. Man you should see those rudders! My arms are awful lame from winding this ole hand wheel all the way from Cincinnati with the rudders all jammed with logs.

Terrible houseboat wind blowing. I have on my neat clean herringbone overhalls and my red shirt and mate's cap.

This is a huge shipyard we're in. Hillman Barge & Construction Co. Big as St. Louis Shipbuilding & Steel Co.

Trierweiler is an O.K. gent. Port engineers always seem to be jolly good fellows while port captains are invariably shits. Well, port captain is a shitty job and I wouldn't take it for all the beer in McKeesport. Ole papa Gilliam (the captain) is one of those old country boys — scared to death of the company — and afraid to order anything we need. But easy to get along with. My status not clarified yet. Probably will go to the easy-handling, beautiful-maneuvering, dirty old Shamrock. *Will miss our lovely quarters and pilot house, but will not have a nervous collapse at each lock. With new*

*rudders and some adjustments to the P. H. controls this tub
might handle, too. Sure is a nice little boat.*

We're 44 miles from Morgantown.

*Say honey, get a couple of cases of beer in the house by the
time I get home will you? Any brand, the funnier the better
— Fountain Brew, Old Style, Peerless, Star.*

*I really feel good this morning. A good night's sleep and
the trip accomplished — and maybe a meal and a show tonight. Can you please learn how to make a puddin like that
we had at the aunts' house?*

*What worried me the most about running nights was, we
had no lifeboat, no anchor line, and no general alarm signal
to the crew quarters. A bad situation.*

Love to you and Superbaby,
Papa.

Well the ole capt. he couldn't stand it so he says to me
"Lissen you are suppose to work when we are in drydock
and help out." I said, "Cap you look on that bulletin board
up on the quarterboat in Joliet, Illinois, where it says who is
on all the boats and under *Brokamp* it says Pilot, Bissell.
That's me. Do you think Mark Twain would get out a chipping hammer and start chipping paint in drydock when he
was a pilot down there in the big bends? No he wouldn't."

"Well that's a poor attitude," he says.

"I was a deckhand long enough to last me a lifetime," I
said.

Well, just to keep peace in the big happy Central Barge
Co. family I went out on deck and looked real interested and
walked around for awhile underneath the boat with a big
stillson wrench in my hand. That satisfied him.

THREE

I Ain't Got no Frog . . .

A good deal too much typewriter ribbon has been chewed to bits by writers chipping away at "The American Frontier." Right this minute there are probably several thousand graduate students pondering the American Frontier and issuing daily manifestos on the subject in order to avoid going to work. It is also on TV every night in the form of endless Westerns and Alaska calls itself "The Last Frontier."

As early as 1893 Frederick Jackson Turner was saying: "And now, four centuries from the discovery of America, at the end of a hundred years of life under the Constitution, the frontier has gone, and with its going has closed the first period of American history."

A scholar named Edwin Fusell goes so far as to say that Mark Twain wasn't even born on the frontier.

Thus, by the time Mark Twain arrived on the scene, the frontier and the West were gone, though their memory left minor, vestigial traces on almost everything he wrote . . .

Neither was Mark Twain born "on the frontier," as so often

alleged, for the frontier, however defined, was in 1835 far west of Florida, Missouri, if, indeed, it was anywhere at all, except as an object of thought or figure of speech . . .

After the Civil War, practically no Americans either knew or cared what they meant by the West, though apparently Mark Twain suspected, for the main point of his role as literary Westerner increasingly came to be its ludicrously anachronistic irrelevance.

All these bold statements are found in Fusell's *American Literature and the American West*.

Bernard De Voto, the late great Harvard scholar in the field of American history and literature, got fed up with the academic open season on the frontier and said, "I have lived in a frontier community and known frontiersmen, as none of the literary folk who now exhibit ideas about frontier life have done."

De Voto came from Utah.

This shot was directed chiefly at Van Wyck Brooks, who, as far as De Voto was concerned, had the wrong slant on nearly everything, despite his fame and success, especially on Mark Twain and notably in his much reviewed, much yakked-about book, *The Ordeal of Mark Twain*.

Brooks came from New Jersey, even from Plainfield.

You may say, if you are paying attention, that I did not come from a frontier town. Well, I did, and what's more Dubuque is still a frontier town. Never mind the K Mart and the new downtown Autobahn that goes noplace and the importation of a few token blacks at the college — going back to Dubuque from the East Coast or the West Coast is like arriving at Dawson on the Klondike in 1899. For one thing you can't ride into town in a passenger train although the population is 80,000 and it is only 185 miles from Chicago. If that's not frontier what is?

Jean Shepherd says, "The thing about the Midwest is that hardly anybody feels part of anything. Everyone is always leaving." That's the frontier. "Faded ambitions and forlorn whistles in the dark." Has nothing to do with "Gunsmoke" and Kitty, the dumbest owner of a saloon in the history of the West. It has nothing to do with wigwams, gunslingers or women in poke bonnets.

The same thing applies to Hannibal as to Dubuque. So I claim Sam Clemens was born and raised on the frontier and his familiarity not only with the frontier but with frontier humor was what gave him his career. He had been raised on the tall story and all those other dreadful sleep-inducing comicalities of the mid-nineteenth-century West and South. He copied it, stole from it, and eventually mastered it. Exaggeration, bumptious behavior, violence, rural innocence, backwoods ignorance, tobacco-juice fun, and anything-for-a-laugh were the rules.

While Henry Adams was hunting for "a world that sensitive and timid natures could regard without a shudder," Mark Twain was out hunting for, and finding, laffs, which brought him money so he could invest it in another perpetual-motion machine.

He found laffs in a lot of easy places. The story that launched him and brought instant notoriety, a typical, long-winded newspaper stuffer called "The Notorious Jumping Frog of Calaveras County," was a well-known story on the West Coast long before Mark Twain got there. William Dean Howells, appropriately the dean of American criticism at the time, and mighty panjandrum of The Boston Literati and hence of The World, said of Mark Twain that this simple public-domain vaudeville exercise was "one of his most stupendous inventions."

Twain didn't invent it but he ran it through the Mark Twain Machine and improved it considerably. Exactly why a frog loaded with buckshot caused the biggest national cackle of the entire nineteenth century is hard, in the age of Johnny Carson, Jack Benny, and Bob Hope, to understand. I suppose frogs are intrinsically funny. Certainly Mr. Toad of *The Wind in the Willows* supplies the main comic element in that sensitive and dreamy fable, and in fact steals the show. Jeremy Fisher, Beatrix Potter's elegantly gaitered frog, is also a funny fellow, especially to look at.

Dragging it out is what makes this story funny if it is funny at all. All that verbosity and shucks-fellers lingo is away out of date now, especially since we are shot down daily by the likes of fast movers like Rodney Dangerfield and Bobby Vernon and David Steinberg, but it holds up pretty well, and it has a nice flurry of dialogue at the end including the line: "Well, I'm only a stranger here, and I ain't got no frog; but if I had a frog, I'd bet you."

I hope you don't break down over that line and get the hiccups and have to drink a glass of water standing on your head; and the likelihood is that you won't. But I like it. After all, Mother has been listening to my brother Mycroft's funny stuff for over a half a century and he hasn't got a laugh out of her yet. Mother says "What are you two laughing about?" so Mycroft goes through it again for her benefit and she says, "Tell me, how are Susan and the children getting along in Harbor Springs?"

On the other hand all her lady friends have always said: "Edith Bissell is a scream," whereas to Mycroft and me her material is a real ho-hum. So that's the way the laff machine works.

Another national howl of the "Jumping Frog" period was Bret Harte's ballad "The Heathen Chinee." The only conclusion we can reach today on reading this deposit of sludge is that everybody back in those days was slightly simple-minded.

Down in the South about the same time that Sam C. was or was not whitewashing that fence in Hannibal, readers of the *Weekly Sunburst* and other such papers were having fits over Johnson J. Hooper's *Adventures of Simon Suggs*. These yawn-producing sketches paved the way for the flood of such japery that clogged up a good deal of the nineteenth century. Mark Twain was raised on it and hugged it to him. He even borrowed from "Simon Suggs Attends a Camp Meeting" — in *Huck Finn*. And the character of the flamboyant Colonel Sellers in *The Gilded Age* was also, partially at least, lifted from Simon Suggs. Well, it worked.

Please note that as early as 1848 the young Sam Clemens was working, at thirteen, in a newspaper office, the Missouri *Courier*, where he had access to all the exchange papers.

Later on in Hartford and Boston, he dressed up in store clothes and had six servants and a coachman but he still liked to play the bumptious irreverent Westerner. It's a great pose, great to play, and *easy*. Easier on the player than the audience. I've been working it for years and it is no trouble at all. For one thing I have a much worse voice than Mark Twain — gravelly, nasal, whiny, just terrible. And I have no "timing" at all, as my theatrical brethren would say. I talk too loud and too fast. The effect is that of a planing mill. This sounds "Western" to people, whereas it is just an accident of nature. Nobody else in the family has an awful voice like this. Little kids in South America follow me down the street trying to make similar noises.

Mark Twain had a Missouri drawl and a superb theatricality in using it. He was a master of the long pause; not as long as Mr. Pinter's people however, and hence highly effective. He also had perfected the dramatic, explosive finish.

Sometimes it is a relief to escape from the hot dry winds of the critical deserts and the loftier prolixity, and hear from a professional. Much has been said of Mark Twain's ability as a lecturer but only by customers and "critics."*

George Arliss, sometimes known as "Disraeli," is at a luncheon given for him by his wife Flo's uncle, Brander Matthews, professor of Dramatic Literature at Columbia University. Arliss, incidentally, was a bit different from the actors and actresses that ramble on in interviews in the Sunday *Times* blissfully intoxicated with self-satisfaction and smugly smothering the reader with teeny weeny notions passing as ideas. Arliss was different in that he could not only speak English, even using multisyllable words, but was a wit and raconteur, and himself wrote plays and books. These talents would have made him a fair curiosity at an Equity meeting today. Back to the luncheon, where we hear one of the greatest actors of his time assess another great exhibitionist and actor. (This is from his autobiography, *Up the Years from Bloomsbury*.)

I shall never forget the thrill I got when I found myself seated next to Mark Twain at luncheon. . . . I believe I have mentioned that my earliest reading was Mark Twain and the Bible. I think I read Mark Twain first. At this luncheon I was more

* John P. Marquand was made fidgety and irritable by book reviewers who called themselves "critics." He said " 'Critics' are nothing but a bunch of ex-obituary writers." Listen, fellows, I don't feel that way. I think critics are swell guys.

fortunate than the others who were present. They were mostly men who had something to say and wanted to say it. Mark arrived in great form; he took the stand and kept it nearly the whole afternoon. I was in luck; I had nothing to say, and more than anything in the world at that moment I wanted to hear Mark Twain talk. He had, as every one knows, a most picturesque head, lit up by those keen and humorous eyes, and decorated with his shaggy hair and brows. But what interested me most was his manner of telling his yarns. Everything he said seemed to be spontaneous, spoken with a slow and fascinating hesitancy. But as the afternoon went on, my experience as an actor told me that there was method in the telling of all his stories; they had been carefully "constructed" so that each point should come in its right place and should lead up to a climax.

Mark Twain was the most popular platform speaker of his time. It was the age of lecture tours and of great humorous elocutionists such as Petroleum V. Nasby and Josh Billings. Everybody was out on the circuit. Bill Nye teamed up with James Whitcomb Riley. Mark Twain hit the road with George Washington Cable. After a few weeks with Cable on the circuit he wrote his wife Livy that Cable was "the pitifulest human louse I have ever known," and also referred to his lecture buddy as "this pious ass" and "this Christ-besprinkled, psalm-singing presbyterian."*

It sometimes seemed as though Mark Twain was forever away on tour. Whenever he needed money, which was always, he lectured his way out of the hole. And after his total bankruptcy in 1894 following the collapse of his publishing house and the final complete and total bustup of his infernal Paige typesetter machine, he climbed aboard again ("the

* Kaplan.

impending horror of the lecture platform") and made a triumphant lecture tour of the U.S.A., Australia, New Zealand, Ceylon, India, and South Africa. By now he was known the world over and the most famous American except for George Washington. The tour was a sensation and a sellout. But it couldn't have been much fun for Sam — sixty years old, bankrupt, crotchety, gnawed by regrets, pawed over by bores, plagued by carbuncles, slightly manic depressive, and loathing travel and the mechanics of travel. "I *hate* travel, and I *hate* hotels."

I love travel and I am crazy about hotels. I will go anyplace, even to Bridgeport, Connecticut, but none of the booking agents ever ask me to go out lecturing. Still, I have had my own modest successes on the platform.

I once gave a lecture to the Dubuque Art Association on "Steamboating in Olden Times on the Upper Mississippi" in conjunction with an exhibit of steamboat paintings by an artist named Bunn. After the lecture Miss Kate van Duzee, a birdlike spinster whose specialty was crayon drawings, said to me, "Richard, I think Mr. Bunn is a very fine draftsman, don't you?" and Mrs. Ella Ruete said she had gone to Keokuk on the steamer *Morningstar* once. Then Mrs. James Burch, who had a lisp, flagged me down and dredged up the following: "I've been to Minneapolith and the room thervith at the Radithon Hotel was unthpeakable." The Dubuque *Telegraph-Herald-and-Times-Journal* said my talk was "witty and informative." Brother Mycroft always referred to it afterwards as "Dick's filibuster on the Steamer *Sprague*."

I also lectured to an English class at the University of Dubuque one time and told them how to go about becoming Famous Writers. This didn't take very well because they all got married later and settled down on Grandview Avenue except one girl who went to Chicago and got pretty high up at Marshall Fields in the chinaware department.

THE LITERARY LIFE

James Joyce to Ezra Pound:
   "Dear Pound: There is nothing phallic about the Blarney stone, so far as I know."

Robert Frost on Ezra Pound:
   "Pound is nuts."

Mark Twain Giving James Fenimore Cooper the Hotfoot

"In Cooper's little box of stage properties he kept six or eight cunning devices, tricks, artifices for his savages and woodsmen to deceive and circumvent each other with, and he was never so happy as when he was working these innocent things and seeing them go. A favorite one was to make a moccasined person tread in the tracks of the moccasined enemy and thus hide his own trail. Cooper wore out barrels and barrels of moccasins in working that trick. Another stage property that he pulled out of his box pretty frequently was his broken twig. He prized his broken twig above all the rest of his effects, and worked it the hardest. It is a restful chapter in any book of his when somebody doesn't step on a dry twig and alarm all the reds and whites for two hundred yards around. Every time a Cooper person is in peril, and absolute silence is worth four dollars a minute, he is sure to step on a dry twig. There may be a hundred handier things to step on, but that wouldn't satisfy Cooper. Cooper requires him to turn out and find a dry twig; and if he can't do it, go and borrow one. In fact, the *Leather Stocking Series* ought to have been called the Broken Twig Series."

FOUR

Not a Difficult Feat,
Even for a Boy

The first boat I built was in our cellar out there on the farm three miles from the Mississippi at the top of the hill above Catfish Creek. Built it nights with my buddy Earl when we were fourteen years old. The teachers called him Earl and the girls who were sweet on him and the rest of us called him Oke because he came up from Oklahoma when he was eight years old. It is tough to have a buddy that can beat you at everything but he could. I was a runt.

His mother had a .45 caliber Oklahoma state trooper's revolver and she could put two holes in a soup can if you threw it in the air. Or one anyway. Actually I don't think she even had a revolver but brother Mycroft started the soup-can legend somehow and then of course we couldn't let it go.

Earl had a young brother we called "the Beaver" because he had a big nose though I don't know what that has to do with beavers. He subsequently went back to Oklahoma and got to be a state trooper.

As for love we were both in love with somebody from eight years on and that included two of the teachers, Clara Bow, and above all Phyllis Haver. Actually I am still in love with Phyllis Haver.

We built that rowboat in the cellar talking about Phyllis Haver and allied subjects dating back to Egyptian times. Earl would kid me about going to dancing class. I liked dancing class just fine but of course I had to pretend to him that I didn't.

"Don't kid me," he would say. "You know you like it, dancing with Billie Jane and her bumps."

"You better look out if you don't wanna good punch in the snoot."

"Who's gonna do it? You awready told me about dancing with Billie Jane, and her bumps, too."

"Aw dry up."

Then my father would come down to throw a few scoops of coal into the furnace and raise hell with the poker and the grates and he would say: "Don't butt those bottom boards up so tight they will swell up and buckle. How is your father, Earl, is he home this week?"

"No, sir, he is on the Road, he is out on the Minnesota territory this week," Oke would say.

"Well he is pushing a very fine line of goods," Father would say and go upstairs and continue reading "Do You Sell Them or Do They Have to Buy?" ("Napoleon was a salesman, Christ was . . .")

Oke even called his own father "sir." I guess that was Southern. His father came from Louisiana and smoked Picayune cigarettes. He moved in an entirely different circle than my father and played poker up on Kimball's Island across from Eagle Point at Doc Pettigrew's cottage, and drank bootleg gin and ginger ale, and knew all sorts of strange people — bootleggers, commercial fishermen, circus people, railroad engineers, sleazy doctors, oil-stock promoters, baseball players . . . and he was not home much of the time.

My father did not drink and resented the rituals of Prohibition-time drinking when Pete Karberg would invite the men out to the pantry before some dinner party and with winks and nudges and remarks about "the real stuff," "right from Canada," etc., he would pour out "a little nip" all around. I suppose Father would take "a little snort to keep the cold out" under those circumstances, but he never kept booze at home and never invited the boys out to the pantry.

After Prohibition Father mellowed a good deal and got whiskey from the Iowa State liquor control for himself and the boys and 89 cent sherry for Mother who never accepted a glass without saying "I'm sure this will make me tipsy."

One time when I was twenty-six years old and Mycroft was twenty-nine, Mother and Father and Mycroft and my wife and I stopped in Guttenberg, Iowa, a very nice old river-town north of Dubuque, on our way down from Lake Superior. "All right boys, let's have a beer," Father said and we went into a saloon and had a 10 cent beer apiece. When we got back to the car Mother said, "Now Fred, you will have to drive, the boys have been drinking."

Guttenberg has some handsome stone houses and a front street right on the river. Dubuque hasn't got that, the river front is all industrial. Guttenberg is also the present home of the former highly precocious Elsie Katzenbach who wrote me an extremely incendiary note in junior high school which my mother found in my pocket. Also the home of Elvira Hedstrom who I was on a double date with one night when Cap Molo managed to run into the East Dubuque bridge abutment. When the cops came he gave his famous imitation of the steamer *Harriet* making a landing in a high wind. But the cops all knew who was who back then and they just told us to go home and not run into the bridge anymore if we could help it.

East Dubuque was a ripsnorter in those days and had

slots, craps, and three or four roulette wheels. It was wide open and three miles from town even had Bonbon McClure's place, a first class whorehouse with girls from Chicago. Bonbon got killed in a fight in East Moline, Illinois. There is still a strip in East Dubuque, with deafening music pits and girls up there wiggling but the gambling is all over. A new governor of Illinois came in on a "Spoil the Fun" ticket, and whether he is still in or not I don't know but the wheels and the merry bouncing of the dice never came back.

And the Hilltop Casino — a tawdry night club of happy memory where the lights burned long, the steaks were tough, the drummer played loud and the MC and the entertainers sweated blood — is gone. When I was home on vacation from steamboating we always headed for East Dubuque and for the Hilltop. The Hilltop was a roadhouse in the best true sense. I often have a crying spell when I think of the nights I have spent half-crocked at Hilltop, looking down the table at my dear friends Tom, Betty, Eddie, Mary, Mycroft, Susie, Courty, Velma, Woody, Jean, Scoop, Heebers, Sis, Marge, John, Angela, Bill, Lenore, Dunc, Pat — that's enough — and across to the minuscule stage where a girl with tassels on her tits is playing a musical staircase with her feet while tossing Indian clubs. Russ Evans is on the drums and giving her all the rim shots she needs. A girl at the next table rotates her head slowly as though it was on a turntable and winks at me. Outside people are "necking" in cars, or possibly "petting." Yes, actually "petting." Gives you goose bumps don't it?

You don't get no goose bumps out of *Oh Calcutta*, just a slight lingering headache.

Twenty-six years after I built my boat, I was a writer and I wrote the book for a Broadway show produced by Boy-Wonder Boy-Millionaire Boy-Producer Hal Prince. He and

I were big old good buddies — he is a very funny guy especially for a producer, and we invited him out to Dubuque one summer when we were there. After I moved away I still kept a houseboat there and I still do, a big steel houseboat 80 feet long.

Hal Prince is a lovely human being but Dubuque is pretty far from Sardi's and I don't think he had a very good time. Dubuque can be very strong medicine for an outsider especially from New York City. And in summer it gets HOT. Mark Twain went to Keokuk, Iowa, in the summer of 1886 to see his aged mother, Jane Clemens. All Sam Clemens had to say about the visit was that it was hot. Keokuk is downriver a ways from Dubuque.

"Keokuk weather was pretty hot. Jean and Clara sat up in bed and cried about it, and so did I. Well it did need cooling; I remember I burnt a hole in my shirt, there, with some ice cream that fell on it."

Hilltop Casino was one of the principal places in Dubuque that Hal Prince didn't really understand. It didn't fit the script, the casting was bad, and all the actors were overboard. But you can't much blame him — it was 95 and 100 degrees all the time he was there in Dubuque and people kept telling him things like "The Langworthy house is the first octagon house west of the Mississippi," and "You wait and see, Iowa is going to beat Minnesota by two touchdowns this year," and brother Mycroft said, "Now you take pompano for example, actually it's not a damn bit better than catfish." So we went to East Dubuque to Eddie Lyons for catfish and, while Hal plucked hopefully at the fish, Eddie sang "Little Sir Echo" in his burlesque-house tenor.

"Listen Hal," Mycroft said, "he knows the guy who wrote that song."

"Who wrote it?" says Hal.

"I don't know," says Mycroft. "Some guy. He knows him. He knows a lot of people in show business. You oughtta talk to him. I'll introduce you."

Then we took Hal to the Dubuque Golf and Country Club and Mycroft introduced him to the bartender. This is one of the highest honors that can come to any visitor to Dubuque. What with the heat and the catfish and "Little Sir Echo" Hal was in kind of a daze by now, and when Eddie Frudden came up and said he knew him from someplace was he in the Navy in 1944, Hal somehow ordered, or got, a sidecar by mistake. So Mycroft started ordering sidecars.

You can't enjoy Dubuque on sidecars, as I have tried it many times and all it got me was a threat of divorce proceedings.

The way you built a boat when I was a kid was to get a book. Nobody was going to show you how, as togetherness in re boat building had not been invented yet. Plenty of togetherness about washing the car and weeding the bean patch but not building a skiff.

My book was *The American Boy's Handy Book* by Dan Beard. In the flyleaf, in a spidery female hand were written the words:

> *Frederick*
> *from*
> *Papa and Mama*
> *January 24, 1890*

My father's twelfth birthday.

This book had been around a long time but it had held up remarkably well considering Father as a boy had got glue on it when making the Giant Chinese Warrior Kite, sawdust in it when he made the Tom Thumb Ice Boat, and paint on page 361 when he constructed the Rainbow Whirlygig. Mycroft and I had also often pummeled it around and left it in the garage and in our tree house but mostly we just looked at it because the projects seemed impossible.

"Procure three twelve inch clear pine boards eighteen feet long . . ."

Now where would we get three pine boards eighteen feet long?

"Next get the blacksmith to make you four iron straps . . ."

WHAT blacksmith? And who was to pay him?

"The grocer will be glad to give you a Chinese tea chest . . ."

Mr. Helbing had a lot of penny candy and Rath's ham sausage but hadn't seen a tea chest since the Spanish American War.

What kind of American Boys were these who could summon up eighteen foot clear pine boards, blacksmiths and tea chests? They were the same kind of boys no doubt who were constantly finding wealthy old gentlemen's pocketbooks in the pages of Horatio Alger, Jr. Horatio Alger was not available at the Carnegie-Stout Public Library under the bluff on 11th Street, but could be procured at the Kresge store at Eighth and Main streets for 10 cents a volume.

But these Horatio Alger heroes all had widowed mothers and a young sister named Nelly to support. If Father had had my interests at heart he would have produced for me a sister named Nelly and left Mother a widow without funds, and by now I would be president of the American Brake Shoe Co.

So neither Mycroft nor I ever dreamed of *making* anything from this book. It was just reading matter, especially the three-story squirrel house with cupola that would "give room for a whole family of squirrels," and the "Boys' Own House-boat," proprietorship of which was as remote from me as that of the Wurlitzer saxophone with pearl keys which sneered at me from the pages of *Boys' Life* every month.

One day after gulping a bit, while Father was reading the *Telegraph-Herald-and-Times-Journal* and smoking a Mela-chrino, I asked him if I could buy a boat. He had just read the daily Abe Martin gem out loud and said "Pretty good."

"Listen Dad," I said, after laughing heartily at Abe Martin which I did not understand why it was funny in the slightest, "can I buy a boat Al Kempf knows a guy who will sell his rowboat for eleven dollars with oars and everything and I have eight dollars in the school savings bank and I can earn some more and this is a real keen boat Al saw it at the Peosta boat club and it is painted red and white and has oars and everything how about it Dad can I buy it huh if I get it I won't even go out on the river I will keep it down on Cat-fish Creek below Swallow Bank and Newton's place gee Dad how about it every kid ought to have a boat it says in *Boys' Life* that owning a boat builds character and just think, if Mark Twain had never had a boat when he was a boy he probly never would have written *Tom Sawyer* and *Life on the Mississippi* can I buy it what about it Dad?"

"How long have you been rehearsing that?" he said.

"Now Fred don't be a tease," Mother said, putting down the *Delineator*.

"Sam Clemens never had a skiff when he was a boy down in Hannibal, they were bone poor. His father was a typical example of a helpless intellectual trapped on the American frontier."

"My father always said he was no gentleman," Mother said.

"Where is my old copy of Dan Beard?" Father said. "Go and get it. Edith, your father as a literary critic leaves something to be desired. Walt Whitman was not a gentleman, Dostoevsky was not a gentleman, Voltaire was not a gentleman, Balzac was not a gentleman, and by your father's standards William Shakespeare was not a gentleman — that is to say he did not eat at Henrici's, play poker at the Chicago Athletic Club, or write letters to the Chicago *Tribune*."

By the time I got back with the book Mother was saying, "I don't think that's a very nice way to talk about my father in front of the boy."

"Your father is all right. I like him," Father said. "Forget about it. Give me the book.

"Now," he said, "the way to get a boat is to make it. Here we are, look at this. 'The Scow. To build a scow-shaped row boat is not a difficult feat, even for a boy. And when it is finished he will find it a very convenient boat, roomy, and not hard to row.' That's the ticket, that's what you want."

"Gee Dad," I said, "I don't know how to make a boat. Will you help me?"

"Not on your life," he said. "But I will foot the lumber bill."

"Crimanentlys," I replied.

And that's how I got my first boat. But we didn't build a scow we built what Dan Beard called a "Yankee Pine," with a pointed bow and some sheer to it. I still have the lumber bill — I throw away *nothing*.

I always kept notebooks, log books, diaries and lists of things I wanted and things I wanted to do sometime. I still have them.

In one of my notebooks for the year 1928 after we built the boat I find the following:

Saturday April 21 —

Embarked at 9:30 AM from Dubuque ice harbor for Dubuque's Grave. Passed steamers *J. W. Weeks* and *C. C. Webber*. Captain Bissell rowing alone. Picked up Al and arrived Catfish Creek 11:30 AM. Beached at Newton's farmhouse picked up Oke rowed up to Rockdale. Tied up. Went to general store for eats and pop. Back to farmhouse. Put stuff in shed and left. Walked home. Al's dog, Sport, with us and Oke's puppy named Buster.

We walked four miles home and were very happy. In this same log book of mine there is a very definite parallel with Mark Twain's desire for command and the right to issue "crisp orders." It says "The captain will have complete authority over his men while in boat *and on way home from boating*."

I am sorry there are no funny boyish misspellings. I know it is against all the rules of boyhood writing but it can't be helped. I was an un-American Boy and a disappointment to everyone because I refused to go along with the Real Boy tradition. I spelled things right and I never played marbles. But don't worry, I chawed tobacker and put rocks in snowballs and did all those other comical things that Real Boys are supposed to do.

That was a nice little boat and it cost 13 dollars for lumber, white lead, cotton, paint, oarlocks and oars. When he was fourteen years old my son Nat said he would shrivel up and die right away if he didn't have a water-ski boat like the other guys. I hate shriveled young people so I quick bought him a boat and it cost me 900 dollars.

Or — —

as Andre Gide said on his deathbed: "Before you quote me, make sure I'm conscious."

FIVE

The House in Faith,
South Dakota

Dubuque, Iowa, on the Upper Mississippi, May, 1927.

MOTHER

Fred, do you think Richard should be allowed to go down and hang around the Mississippi River?

(Mother never said "the river" like other people, she gave it the full treatment to make it sound more ominous. Because wasn't it the biggest river in the world? Unfortunately she had a point, for every year about a dozen people in the area managed to get themselves drowned in it. On one occasion a hobo accomplished it the hard way by falling off a boxcar on the East Dubuque railroad bridge into the river, no mean feat.)

RICHARD (*a lively lad of fourteen*)

I don't hang around the river. I study it. There's a lot of history in that ole harbor.

MOTHER

Yes and hobos behind Jackson's peanut butter factory, too.
And all those railroad tracks and that steam thing of Molo's.
(What ever happened to "hobos" anyway? I haven't seen
Weary Willie or Dusty Rhoades in years.)

RICHARD

Gee Mum, that's just a steam crane unloads the sand from
barges. How could that hurt anybody unless they climbed
on top of it and jumped off? Gee whiz.

FATHER

Watch that tone of voice, young man. Edith, this egg is not
fit to eat.

MOTHER

I'm not surprised. She didn't come in until after midnight.
Dance, dance, dance. I never knew there were so many
dances until she came to work for us.

RICHARD

(*gaining points by eating some glutinous cereal called
Wheatola*) How about it, Dad?

FATHER

How about what?

MOTHER

Fred, I wish you would put down that paper and cooperate. He wants to go down to the Mississippi River with his chum. (Mother used words like "chum" and "beau.")

FATHER

Well it's all right with me. . . . This young Lindbergh is out to kill himself. Smart aleck says he is going to fly across the Atlantic all alone in a single engine plane. Darn chump.

RICHARD

Yay bo! Thanks Dad! Yay! Keen!

MOTHER

Oh I wish we could have some dignity at the breakfast table.

FATHER

I used to go out in a skiff from Bisbings' Springs and ride the log rafts. The raftsmen out of Black River were the roughest element on earth. They all carried bowie knives and when they were in liquor would just as soon kill a man as give him the time of day.

RICHARD

Golly, Dad, did you ever talk to a real Black River raftsman?

FATHER

Certainly. Lots of times. They enjoyed our company. One of them gave me an apple one time. Big brute must have stood six-foot-five. "Study your books, sonny," he said, "and you won't never have to go arafting."

RICHARD

Boyoboy. I'd *like* to go arafting. Can I have a dime for carfare?

FATHER

You mean, can I have a nickel for carfare and a nickel for a Coney Island hot dog covered with chili and Lord knows what. All right, if you are determined to have stomach ulcers before you are twenty, here's a quarter. Treat your friend Oke and have a bottle of Cosley's soda pop. Come over to the factory and I'll give you a ride home and you'll have a nickel to spare.

MOTHER

I don't know what we're coming to.

When there was vaudeville, "Dubuque" was a good joke like "Peoria," "Walla Walla," and in New England "Fitchburg." It is still considered pretty comical in some quarters and over the years I've taken a lot of jug-headed ribbing about it. Then there's that hoary old saw about the *New Yorker* and the "little old lady from Dubuque." Only last

year a Feature Writer was dispatched from the lordly New
York *Times* to hunt up the typical "Old Lady from Dubuque" (chuckle). The resulting gruel was as tasty as library paste but no doubt entertained the Little Old Lady
from New Rochelle, the Little Old Lady from Rivington
Street, and the Little Old Lady from Lenox Avenue.

No former New Yorkers live in Dubuque so far as I know,
but several former Dubuquers live in New York. When they
come home to Dubuque it starts out O.K. but soon turns
embarrassing and they hurry back to Fun City to join in the
fun again.

The mystique of Dubuque is so powerful that when you
come back from being away you get all fussed up even when
you are still in Chicago waiting in the cattle pen at the Ozark
Airlines. Seized with cold sweats and clammy palms you
have visions of painful confrontations at the Golf Club,
lapses in conversation with people whose names you can't
remember, meaningless circular dialogues with relations,
the inevitable necrology, the nonstop drinking, the invita-
tions, the enormous steaks . . . Mother . . . ("Go out to
the kitchen, Richard, and speak to Frieda.")

But when you get out of the plane there is Mycroft and
Susie and Eddie and Mary or Dunc and Pat and you go right
over the bridge to East Dubuque and stop at the liquor store
and the girl there says, "Hi Dick, how long you here for this
time? I spose you're going down to the river."

Then we are on Charlie Vandermillen's boat dock and
Charlie is there in hip boots and some ducks are walking
around on the float. There's that great Mississippi River
smell which foreigners don't understand, and a dead carp
floating around.

So you all get in Mycroft's boat and go over to his houseboat. And everything is all right.

It's hard to grow old, Huckleberry, and see the steamboats go down, and the one cylinder Scheppele engines, and the trolley cars, the roller coaster, the St. George and the Page hotels, and good old Jazzbo . . . but the river is still there, and the willows, and the riprap, and the Mormon flies in June piled under the street lamps near the river on South Main Street. All the bright talents of the Urban Renewal demolition squads have been unable to quash the annual advent of the Mormon flies from the river. There they swirl in swarms around the street lamps, there they lie in drifts along the sidewalks, wiggling and squirming as they perish in wormy disarray. It must make the Urban Renewal gents mad enough to stamp their feet and cry, "Oh prunes!"

I met a lady at a cocktail party last year in New York and she said "You come from Iowa don't you? I went through Iowa last summer. It's a beautiful state."

So I sang the Iowa Corn Song and got quite a hand.

So then we all had to be quiet while the composer played and sang the songs for a new musical comedy. There were quite a few Beautiful People there and while I nodded and smiled and applauded I was thinking of Dubuque, and the river and Mr. Bingham's boathouse, and the yard at the Dubuque Boat and Boiler Co. (Incidentally that was the end of that musical comedy. It went down shortly afterwards with all hands still singing.)

Mr. Bingham was the Vice President of "Glovers," my father's firm, of which Father was General Manager when I was a kid, and Grandfather, President. This was a wholesale house and garment manufacturing concern of awesome longevity, sublime virtue, and declining sales. "Glovers" was the first garment manufacturing plant west of the Mississippi. They made work garments and old Mr. John Glover patented the "Glover overall." In some dusty back room in some small town store in North Dakota I feel sure there lies today an antique sample of this extinct species. Probably a size 52 and that's why it didn't sell all these years.

My Grandfather, in true Horatio Alger style, had risen From Office Boy to President. "Glovers" built Grandfather's elegant manse on West Third Street, in 1891, with its open stair well, lavish woodwork and billiard room and Dutch paintings of cows. "Glovers" sent Father to Exeter and Harvard and "the girls" to Bryn Mawr. "Glovers" took them all to Europe, and to the Drake in Chicago for the opera to hear Mary Garden and Martinelli, and to Glacier Park, and to Morro Castle in Havana. "Glovers" bought the Hudson limousine, and John Werner the chauffeur. "Glovers" footed the bill for a houseman named Sesto Raspellini, for the Steinway and sets of china and golf clubs and Havana cigars and for things from Marshall Fields and A. Starr Best.

"Glovers" was only three blocks from the river and from the cutting room on the fifth floor you could look across certain drab rooftops to the harbor and clear out to the channel. When I worked there I used to go up to the cutting room to "check up on things" a dozen times a day. "Checking up" consisted of talking to the cutting foreman for two minutes and gazing at the harbor and the river for ten minutes.

Mr. Bingham's boathouse contained an antique cabin launch called the *Clytie* with an enormous gas engine which was started by putting a bar to the flywheel. Mr. Bingham's boathouse smelled of oily rags and fish. There was always a dead carp floating in the slip beside the boat when you entered the boathouse and the first thing to do was to get an oar and steer it out of the slip into the harbor. The fish knew his business and would float next door and into Mr. Cliff Sheffield's boathouse.

The river was somehow a part of the firm as it was a part

of the town. Down at the end of Third Street by the Star
Brewery was the railroad drawbridge and when the boats
blew for the draw you could hear them plainly right in the
office. It often made me sad, lonely, distracted, and nervous.
At the time of the big spring floods the river came right up
the street and into the basements of the Glover buildings.
Then there was a big hullabaloo moving piece goods and
buttons and cases of thread out of the basements — and
manning the pumps.

Dubuque was a real rivertown and there is nothing quite
like it. Any rivertown is better than any no-river town but
this was the Mississippi, the real stuff. It was inconvenient,
but somehow there was some glory in having the Father of
Waters in your basement.

Mark Twain shortchanged Dubuque woefully in *Life on
the Mississippi*. He took a trip to St. Paul in 1882 to gather
material — any kind of stuffing would do — with which to
pad out the original manuscript, which had appeared in the
Atlantic Monthly, from three hundred pages to a book length
of six hundred pages. The book was to be a "subscription
book," sold by door-to-door salesmen for parlor display, and
had to be big and heavy and impressive. Mark Twain managed to blow it up to 624 pages and my copy weighs nearly
3 lbs. The last part of the book is a real pile of sawdust.

It was the kind of a work outing he detested and he de-
scribed the trip as "hideous." The copy that came out of this
is an embarrassing farrago betraying a dogged determina-
tion to put it down somehow and get it over with.

Of Dubuque, the fabled, wondrous gem of the Upper
Mississippi, he can only set down a few static phrases which
seem to have been copied out of Colton's *Guide for Emi-
grants* or a school geography.

"Dubuque is situated in a rich mineral region. The lead

mines are very productive, and of wide extent. Dubuque has a great number of manufacturing establishments; among them a plough factory which has for customers all Christendom in general."*

He then cooks up a regular sinker of a joker about the plough which is too sad for words. That's all.

At least half of *Life on the Mississippi* is expendable and the consistency of raisin pie from the railroad depot lunch counter.

Father ruled the firm with an iron hand.

Father was fond of Business Conferences.

There were several forms of the Business Conference. Take the year 1938.

Father, who was president by then, would call a conference in his private office which had on the wall a framed certificate from the U.S. Patent Office issued to our firm in 1882 for a patent bib overall which we had ceased manufacturing in 1911. There was a large picture of the Roman Forum, one of Teddy Roosevelt, and a buffalo skull from Father's trip to Wyoming in 1898. Besides Father's desk and swivel chair there were six straight-back chairs against two walls. Mother finally persuaded Father to buy a new dining room set on a trip to Chicago in 1925. These six black-oak executives' chairs were Mother's old dining room chairs and nobody thought there was anything funny about it either.

One chief type of conference was for Father to summon Pete Karberg, Con Birkness, Walter Blades, Presley Fawkes (who was then eighty-two years old and sharp as a tack), and me into the private office.

"Shut the door, Richard," was the first piece of business.

---

* This was the "Norwegian Plow Co.," long gone from the scene.

Father would then quote from the Kiplinger letter from Washington, and then cuss Franklin Delano Roosevelt and predict his downfall until lunchtime. Father went home to lunch, the other executives would go to lunch at Ernie Kretz's Cafeteria on Main Street, and I would go across the street and eat in our factory lunch room because I was in love with a brunette label paster and she would be eating there with Jeanie Palm and Katie Bargen, and we could look at each other.

Another popular conference was the Sales Conference. This consisted of calling Alan Graves, Con Birkness, Karberg, Bill Kaynor, and me into the office.

"Shut the door, Richard."

Father would then wave some of the morning's orders in the air and want to know why Leo Cassidy had only sold a bill for fall of $185 to our fine old loyal customer Solkowsky, Glutzbach and Klaussen (real name).

"It's the paved roads and the automobile," Karberg would say.

"J. C. Penney," Kaynor would say.

"Sears Roebuck," Con Birkness would say.

"Farm prices," Presley Fawkes would say.

"Frank Schmidt used to sell them bills of over two thousand dollars for fall," Father would say. "It's that damn Roosevelt."

I would go to the window to "let in a little air" but actually to look across the street at the brunette label paster who pasted labels on boxes at a table by a window directly across the street in our other building. Sometimes she would give me a little finger-wiggling wave.

"If you would give me a wool and suede zipper jacket to retail for three ninety-five, I could sell them three hundred units," Con Birkness would say. He was raised in the Dakotas and had an accent like Lawrence Welk. He couldn't say "zipper" he said "sipper." A "zipper jacket" was a "sipper chacket."

"Next I suppose you'll be telling me about Butler Brothers," Father would say with a fiendish Yankee sneer.

Father hated Butler Bros., Sears Roebuck, Montgomery Ward, and Franklin Delano Roosevelt about the same. They were none of them to be trusted, they cut prices and skimped their patterns, even F.D.R. Deep in his soul also lurked a pained frenzy about F.D.R.'s mother. Not Eleanor, old Sarah. My father's family were Iowa pioneers and came long ago from a farm in upstate New York. Maybe the cold winters had something to do with our obsessions. Maybe it was just that ornery Yankee strain.

That's about it on the Sales Conference only it went on for hours, sometimes days, and Wilson Bros., McGregor, and Cluett Peabody got plenty lumps.

About twice a year we would have a Directors' Meeting on the subject: "What shall we do with the house in Faith, South Dakota?"

In the dim past we had acquired, on a bad debt, a frame house in the tiny prairie town of Faith, S.D. A local agent rented it for us and these meetings were to discuss whether to continue renting the house, for $16 a month, or to sell it.

Many years later, long after I had left the firm, I met Presley Fawkes striding down West Third Street. He was then ninety-six and hale, as they say, and hearty.

"How about the house in Faith, South Dakota?" I asked him after he had given me his detailed opinion of the week's movements on the New York Stock Exchange.

"We just sold it," he said. "I told them we should keep renting it but they wouldn't listen to me."

There was also the Style Conference which took place in the Sample Room. This went on for several days with the air filled with flying swatches, bolts of cloth, cost sheets, and sample garments.

We had increased our problems by invading the highly competitive field of men's pajamas. So on occasion I was called on to model some hot new number in the line in Father's private office. Later on, the brunette label paster would say to me, "You looked real cute in those pajamas this morning."

Father was always determined to prove that all our competitors skimped on their sizing. Now there is a way of making *any* garment look too short in the sleeves. If you throw your shoulders back and stretch your arms way out, the sleeves will ride up and look too short.

We would have a pair of Wilson Bros. pajamas under analysis, bought at retail up at Roshek's or Ed Graham's store, and I would be modeling them.

"What do you think of their sizing, Frank?" Father would say to Frank Fox, our stylist.

"Well, not so bad," Frank would say. "Now they've got this pattern exclusive from Galey and Lord . . ."

"That garment looks skimped to me," Father would say. "Here, let me try that on."

So he would take his coat off and put the pajama coat on over his shirt and tie and throw his shoulders back and stretch his arms out and the sleeves would ride up and Father would say, "What did I tell you? Look at those sleeves."

I was in it for sixteen years, both before and after I went off steamboating. Pilots, engineers, and mates off the river used to appear at the factory, looking unnatural in their shore clothes, and I would take them up into stock and sell them a jacket or a sheep-lined coat or some shirts at whole-sale. They used to say "How can you stand it working inside?"

Father kept at it until he was in his eighties and, since he wouldn't go home, the stockholders shut the doors, after ninety-nine years in business.

The brunette label paster went to Southern California and got married.

Office, factory, and warehouse were blasted to the level earth during the recent period of pestilential blight known as Urban Renewal.

Mr. Bingham's boathouse is gone too, but a dead carp is floating around on the site. I often wonder how Oscar Hammerstein wrote all those lyrics for "Old Man River" without getting a dead carp in there someplace.

SIX

Results of Dancing on Sunday

What was it like on the Upper Mississippi when my grandfather was a young man? Pretty much the way you would expect, except maybe that some little random points of view that you wouldn't think of have changed in a hundred years. Like the connection between dancing on Sunday and tornados.

From that great, long-out-of-print classic, *Old Times on the Upper Mississippi* by George Byron Merrick,* we bring you for the first time in reprint a tale from the long ago including a splendid sample of Captain Merrick's witty style:

Captain William Fisher, of Galena, Illinois, is probably the oldest living pilot of the Upper Mississippi. At the time of this writing (1908), he is spending the closing years of his life in quiet comfort in a spot where he can look down upon the waters of "Fevre" River, once alive with steamboats, in the pilot houses of which he spent over thirty years in hard and perilous service.

Two or three incidents of his river life are of interest, as showing the dangers of that life . . .

"The next year I was engaged on the *Alex. Mitchell*. We had

---

* I paid $14.50 for my copy years ago. It has now soared to $95 on the antiquarian book market, which has gone crazy along with everything else.

left St. Paul at 11 o'clock in the forenoon, on Saturday, May 6, 1872. I am particular about this day and date, for the point of this story hinges on the day of the week (Sunday). In trying to run the Hastings bridge we were struck by a squall that threw us against the abutment, tearing off a portion of our starboard guard. We arrived at La Crosse, Sunday morning, and took on two hundred excursionists for Lansing. They wanted to dance, but it being Sunday Captain Laughton hesitated for some time about giving them permission, as it was contrary to the known wishes, if not the rules, of Commodore Davidson to have dancing or games on board of his boats on Sunday. The passengers were persistent, however, and at last Captain Laughton yielded, saying that he couldn't help it! Of course he might have helped it. What is a captain for, if not to run his boat, no matter if everybody else is against him? That was where he was weak. He finally yielded, however and they danced all the way to Lansing. When we arrived there it was raining, and the excursionists chartered the boat for a run back to Victory, about ten miles, and they were dancing all the time.

"Leaving them at Victory we proceeded on our way down the river. When about twelve miles above Dubuque, a little below Wells's Landing, at three o'clock Monday morning, we were struck by a cyclone. We lost both chimneys, the pilot house was unroofed, and part of the hurricane deck on the port side was blown off. Mr. Trudell, the mate, was on watch, and standing on the roof by the big bell. He was blown off, and landed on shore a quarter of a mile away, but sustained no serious injuries. The port lifeboat was blown a mile and a half into the country. Following so soon after the Sunday dancing, I have always felt that there was some connection between the two."

Captain Fisher is a very conscientious man — a religious man, and he believes in observing Sunday — that is, keeping it as nearly as is possible on a steamboat running seven days in the week. The dancing was wholly unnecessary, if not in itself immoral, and its permission by Captain Laughton was in direct contravention of the known wishes if not orders of the owners.

Hence the conclusion that Providence took a hand in the matter and meted out swift punishment for the misdoing. I did not argue the matter with the captain; but I could not reconcile the unroofing of Commodore Davidson's steamboat, or the blowing away of Mr. Trudell, who had no voice in granting license to the ungodly dancers, with the ordinary conception of the eternal fitness of things. If it had blown Captain Laughton a mile and a half into the country, as it did the port lifeboat, or even a quarter of a mile, as it did Mr. Trudell, and had left Commodore Davidson's steamboat intact, the hand of Providence would have appeared more plainly in the case. As it was, Captain Laughton slept serenely in his berth while Mr. Trudell and the lifeboat were sailing into space, and he did not get out until all was over. It is pleasant to be able to relate that although Providence appears to have miscarried in dealing out retribution, Commodore Davidson did not. Captain Davis was put in charge of the *Alex. Mitchell* as soon as she struck the levee at St. Louis.

SEVEN

Send Me Two Dollars.
I Have Three Cents.

In 1937 I made a couple of trips to the Mediterranean as ordinary seaman on the American Export Line and I learned about the sea and about French women, Italian women, Greek women, Syrian women, Nubian women, Egyptian women, and I had my picture taken, in my romantic seafaring togs, in front of the Porch of the Maidens on the Acropolis. Then I decked for a while on the Upper Mississippi on the *James W. Good*, big sternwheel steamer of the Federal Barge Lines, but the trouble with the *James W. Good* was that I wanted to get married and I couldn't see how I could get married on $52.50 a month. So I went ashore and went to work for Father at Glovers (see "Business Conferences") and he started me at $15 a week, which wasn't much improvement as on the barge line I was getting room and board free. Well, I stuck it out and got married when my salary got to $22.50 a week.

When the war came along I went back to steamboating, for the Central Barge Co. of Chicago whose marine headquarters were at Joliet, Illinois, on the Des Plaines River, which connected with Chicago, 33 miles away, by the Chicago Sanitary and Ship Canal. Fifteen miles south, the Des Plaines joined the Kankakee to form the Illinois River which empties into the Mississippi at Grafton, above St. Louis. We were towing coal from Havana, Illinois, to the Commonwealth Edison Company power plants in Chicago. From Havana to Joliet the big boats usually brought up eight barges at a time, about 9,600 tons. At Joliet the barge tows were broken up and the little boats took them up the Drainage Canal in smaller units, right up past the Chicago Opera House, the Union Station, and Wacker Drive. All this may be boring but that's the way it was and they put me on the *Wheelock Whitney.* I decked on the Illinois and on the Mississippi and was a Good Boy and in the course of time I got to be Second Mate.

Actual Life on the Illinois River— The Flood

Peoria, Illinois
April 14, 1943

Dearest Wife:
We have been doing rescue work and flood work and have all been on watch about 72 hours catching an hour nap here and there when we can. Spotting U.S. Engineer Dept. dredge #201 which is loading barges with river sand, and then we spot the barges up and down the levees where gangs are filling sand bags and battening levees. Capt. Ingersoll aboard. I was sounding with the lead line tonight and got 38 ft. right off shore by the Hiram Walker distillery. The whole damn town is out working. Traffic from the East is shut off. All railroad bridges below here out of commission. Exciting time and you know us boys we like the excitement.

This is some flood — *worst since 1844. We are the only boat still operating here on the Illinois except small U.S. Engineer Dept. launches. All Central, Federal, Mechling, Falcon and Ohio River Co. boats tied up. We're ready all the time to abandon ship — lifeboats ready, preservers etc. so don't worry. They broadcast about us on the radio today — valiant* Wheelock Whitney, *plucky crew etc. The water is lapping at the tops of the dikes and every time we shove a barge up against the dike it's a question whether we knock a hole in the levee and that would be The End. We had refugees all over the boat down below Peoria filling them up with coffee etc. Their homes and farms are completely out of sight. We been working trying to save dikes around Caterpillar plant all day (they make Army tanks etc.). We were spotting sand barges for about 800 workers. It has cost this one plant alone 2,000,000 dollars already. Our bill for towing charges for just last three days is $4,000. And god damn it we have five loads of Havana coal tied off in the woods below Pekin. Copperas Creek out of sight. Boy it's exciting. Big loudspeakers mounted all over so you can hear announcements such as "Send a new squad of men to the dike below Cedar Street bridge. It is getting spongy," and "Will the* Wheelock Whitney *move the Dredge number 201 at once. They are running out of sand." These statements coming booming out at all hours of the day and night. Capt. Ingersoll treated me fine. He asked Frosty how I was doing and Frosty said I was a big improvement over the last second mate and I was doing lots better than them dumb farmer mates out of the bushes. I'm tired. Peoria lock disappeared. Starved Rock lock out and Peoria bridges knocked out so we can not go north anyway. No barges loading at Alton so no use to go there either.*

　　Things are worse they say down at Beardstown tonight but they are fighting inch by inch. Cook is doing a great job feeding us, Army men, strays, reporters, the mayor, and various visiting givers of lousy advice. Being on top of a real flood is a strange experience. More rain. It is sad to see these people who have lost their homes, machinery and crops looking up at the sky to see more rain. I have no idea what day this is.

Later: we are still at it tooth and nail. We have to get some rest soon and will start standing watches. Dave wrote his wife: "Honey you better get a good look at the floors and the walls because when I get home all you're going to see is the ceiling. You know what I mean, honey. Ha ha."

I think we have got her licked. The smell from the distilleries here is awful. Signed on some new boys last week (I am clerk again now as well as 2nd mate; 50 cents a day to do logs and all ships business.) I found two guys who had no idea how their wives' names were spelled, one who didn't know how to spell the name of his hometown, and two who didn't know on what street they lived. Things haven't changed much since Huck Finn and Co.

Radio says flood is cresting Thank God.

The Food on the Illinois

Above Havana, Ill., coming up with eight loads coal for Chicago on a hot day.

BREAKFAST	LUNCH
French toast	Baby green onions
Sausages	Garden salad
Fried eggs	Sliced iced new tomatoes
All kinds dry cereal	Spare ribs of beef
Oatmeal	Mashed potatoes
Coffee Tea Milk	Creamed corn

Baby lima beans
White, rye, graham bread
Tea   Coffee   Cold milk or
   Ice water
All sauces, A-1, L&P, salad
   dressings, jams

SUPPER
East St. Louis salad
Roast pork
Spaghetti
Baked beans home baked
   with pork
Scalloped potatoes
Mashed potatoes
Creamed asparagus
Hot biscuits
Fruit Jello
Assorted cookies
Iced tea etc.

EVENING LUNCH 9 P.M.
Apples, oranges
Hard boiled eggs
Munster cheese
American cheese
Head cheese
Oscar Mayers liver sausage
Bologna sausage
Ham sausage
Asst. breads
Cold supper biscuits
Jams, peanut butter, peach
   preserves
Krispy crackers
Cookies, slab cake etc.
Tea   Coffee   Milk (also
   Cocoa — Coffee half and
   half)

Personal Problems on the Illinois

"Send my slippers to Joliet. I need them off watch."

"I feel better as soon as I get away from the quarterboat and Joliet and off down the river."

"I don't think I am going to sour on Dewey Murphy. I think he is untouched by the usual emotions that make so many pilots and captains turn into craps. Same goes for Gene W. and Chuck Partridge."

"Honey please send me 2 dollars I haven't enough money for tobacco. I have 3 cents."

"We got a new case of cookies but no yellow elastic marshmallow type this time."

"Your letter came. This ornery new mate says to me 'Bissell get off your ass and see what them god damn deckhands is doing. And oh yeah, here's a letter for you.' I lie awake hating this bastard like Sam Clemens did that pilot named Brown."

"It's Sunday and we are going down with MTs and picnickers are under the trees along the way, girls in transparent dresses waving from bridges, cows munching, wild roses on the banks — fairly makes me wild to get off and roll in the June grass."

"I had a chance to buy another knife so I did. I'll sell it to somebody and make 50¢ on it. Knives are scarce."

"Oh my damn shoe is splitting again — up the goddam back this time."

"Went out on the head of the barges tonight to set the running lights. The off watch was out there and that kid wiper from the engine room had his guitar and he was singing them old-time songs. Three minutes later I was homesick like somebody stuck a knife in me."

"I love you baby . . ."

"Send me some stamps."

After Raising the Sunken Towboat Glenn Traer when She Hit the Marseilles Dam

June 5, 1943
Joliet Illinois
Des Plaines River

They raised the Traer *and towed her up to Joliet and we are tied alongside and I am stealing everything in sight off of her for our boat. It is the same company so it is not really stealing. Did you ever notice how everybody in that swell kids' book* Huck Finn *is always stealing things — skiffs, chickens, watermelons, sweet corn, apple pies, shirts, bedsheets, spoons, money, pie pans, everything they can lay their hands on. When I bummed the freights up with Al K. and rowed down from Winona Minn. that time when I was a kid I stole that rowboat. After reading Huckleberry I figured it was expected of me, normal conduct.*

So far I have swiped a complete set of bitts worth $8.95, 3 ratchets at $75 apiece, 12 gallons of paint, 3 high class wood chisels, 14 cold shuts, 2 axes — all of which I need here for our own work. They will have to refit anyway so it's everybody for himself. Schibrowsky says Sibley has quit result of the sinking but I doubt old jingle jangle would do that. We are of course cleaning up the Traer *there was two of the crew drowned in their bunks when they raised her but we had nothing to do with that. Yesterday they sent me and Raymond one of the deckhands down in the hold to clear out the deep freeze. It was all filled with a couple of hundred pounds of chickens and cuts of meat. Of course it has not been running since she sank ten days ago so you can imagine the smell when I lifted that lid. I closed it pretty soon but* *not soon enough for Raymond began to heave just to add to the fun. I went up and told them they would have to get somebody else on that job. So nobody would go down. Today the Coast Guard boat was alongside and I went over and asked them if they had any gas masks would they lend us a couple. That's how we got that rotten meat out, passing it up in buckets and the guys on deck dumped it in the river. Only good thing is, I salvaged 30 two lb. cans of coffee lodged in the mud in the engine room. Chase and Sanborns.*

Here is a hunk out of a letter I found all mashed up in the gutter by the saloon (two blocks away) — why do I look in gutters?

"And when he came in he says I know you was out with somebody else last night theys no movie shows that lasts till 12 midnight. Oh honey I wanted so to tell him sure I was out with somebody that really loves me and oh honey how can I go on without you near me he is such a mistake and you are so young and wonderful." It was addressed to that good lookin sheik junior engineer we have got on here now that was in the Navy.

Captain Hillman said to Frosty, "We are getting out of here tomorrow." Frosty said, "You better look out the boat don't sink. Bissell and his deckhands has lifted everything off the Traer *but the engines."*

Believe me sweetheart we will all be glad to get out of Joliet and off down the river.

Will be home in 13 days please meet me in East Dubuque with the baby. If nobody will bring you get a Black & White cab.

Violence on the Illinois River

"Scotty says Pappy R. pulled a knife on Murdock over at the Paradise and cut his stomach open till his guts were sticking out. Murdock had a close call would have died only they got him to the hospital in 15 mins."

"Got put on the *Keeneland* for a trip into Chicago. Never been on this run before and it's no good. There is a new pilot on there one of the most miserable bastards I ever met on the river and he kept humiliating and chewing out this one deckhand until this kid picked up a shackle laying on the stern end of the barge and threw it right through the pilot house window."

Going Aground on the Illinois River

Towboats were scarce because the shipyards were making practically nothing but Navy and Army boats. The company needed more power so the Army sent us two tugboats on charter. These had model hulls and were not designed for pushing barges they were just regular hawser tugs. They were hard to handle when hooked up somehow and when backing were likely to go any which way.

Illinois River
D.P.C. #67
Dec. 7, 1943

Dearest M —
    We went hard aground yesterday below Ottawa, bam! boom! and the boat piled up in the stumps. I ran up to the pilot house hell bent and expecting pilot in hysterics but all

Pappy said was "Well, here we are, brother Biss." Captain Chuck was down playing poker and after finishing the hand *he come on up and said "I guess there is nothing we can do untwil another boat comes" and he went back down to the poker game. Pappy says "I guess I will join that game. Brother Biss get a spike pole and sound around the boat see how much water we got." The boat was all tipped over at a mean angle and I got only 3 feet on starboard side.*

They played poker from 4:15 to 5:30, ate supper, and then Capt. Chuck rowed over to a farmhouse and called Lynn Childs in Chgo. and told him we was on the stumps. At 7:30 PM old DPC 68 come creeping up with 4 loads and we had a tugging party and she finally hauled us off ground after tipping us over so far all the bottles of vinegar, mustard, ketchup, syrup, honey, hot sauce, Worcestershire, marmalade, plum butter etc. all fell out of the cupboards onto the deck of the galley. I went to bed.

When I came on at midnight we were aground again and our tow was crosswise in the Peru bridge — I had to climb up on the bridge sheer fence with a lock line so we could work against it. Below the bridge there was another towboat.

"That's the Whitney," *says Capt. Chuck. "She's aground too."*

This morning we got stuck in some gooey mud below Pekin and had to break our tow to get turned around. These DPC boats have no backing rudders. I have been doing lots of steering for Pappy while he plays poker but I haven't put her aground yet but then, I haven't had to back her down any.

I sure got a laugh out of that grounding yesterday on Delbridge Island. Any other C.B. Co. boat I ever worked on the pilot and captain would have had fits. Except Winslow I guess.

Winter on the Illinois River

"It is ten below zero and a wind howling down from Lake Michigan. The lock gates are jammed with ice cakes and we have to fish and poke them out with pike poles. The lines freeze to the timberheads and we have to beat them with axes. We put the lock lines under canvas with kerosene lanterns underneath to keep them limber but it doesn't do much good. Just think, I could go A.B. on the Grace Line and be in Callao or Valparaiso tonight. I guess I am not too smart."

Humor on the Illinois River not Derived from Mark Twain, Who Let His Wife Edit His Stuff

"It cost me seventy bucks," I says to Duke, "to get my wife over here from home."

He says "You fool you could have gone down to The Elms and got a good piece for two dollars."

"I'll tell my wife what you said," I says.

And he says "You won't dass to."

I says "Oh the hell I won't," and I told her, sure enough.

"I'll 'good piece' him," she says, and next morning she come down to the boat.

"Where is that Duke ahidin at?" she says. "I have got a bone to pick with him."

Ole Duke I seen him ascootin around a corner and he stayed hid all the time she was there, ahidin from her.

EIGHT

Drink a Luxury and Vice an Entertainment

The Tennessee River is the largest branch of the Ohio. It starts about four miles from Knoxville, rolls southwestward through Tennessee, gurgles into Alabama, makes a big curve and swashes northward crossing the entire state of Tennessee for the second time, and makes a run for it north through Kentucky and dumps into the Beautiful Ohio at unbeautiful Paducah. In the course of this careless vagrancy, the Tennessee River runs up a total bill of 652 miles.

We were running from Evansville, Indiana, down the Ohio to the mouth of the Tennessee at Paducah, and up the Tennessee to Sheffield, Alabama. This was about a 400 mile run. One hundred and fifty miles on the Ohio and 250 miles on the Tennessee. We were on an old-style, coal-burning, hand-fired, high-pressure sternwheel steamboat, the *Minnesota*. This boat hadn't been built for towing, everything was going wrong, and it was my first job on the river as mate. We had brought her all the way down from the Illinois River and we were in a foreign land — the South. More than that, we were on a nineteenth-century river that flowed through

Kentucky, rural Alabama and Tennessee. The year was 1942 but up this valley it was 1868, it was 1896, it was 1910.

It was being down on the Tennessee and for several days we had been quarreling with the river, which was full and intent on shoving us right back down to W. L. Berry Light and the Ohio. We had to double trip at Duck River Suck and at Petticoat Riffle, and if those names aren't alluring enough and evocative enough of saddle-bag cabins and hound dogs, I'll tell you some more, because the nomenclature of the rivers and the crossroads of the South is a pretty rich gumbo.

"What is this crop?" I asked Lee Roy the deckhand when we were up at the top of the bank on the edge of a field hunting for a tree to tie off to.

"That there is peanuts," he said. "Don't you grow no peanuts up there?"

By "up there" he meant up North, up in those outlandish nations above the Ohio.

"No, we don't grow no peanuts, we grow corn mostly. Now, Lee Roy what is this here vine I see all over with the big leaves?"

"Why Cap, dog take it, that's *kudzu*. Don't tell me you ain't got no *kudzu* up there?"

The next night we came up to Pittsburg Landing on the west bank and we tied up on account of fog. We were running into a good bit of surface fog these nights down on the river because it was the fall of the year. Pittsburg Landing, Tennessee, was the scene for one of the big glorious blood baths of history, called the Battle of Shiloh.

I went off watch at midnight and ambled into the galley and the deckhands and the second mate and the pilot and the engineer and the cook, who had insomnia, were all setting around eating, and drinking coffee.

"Cap," I said to the old, old trip pilot we had aboard, "where is that battlefield at?"

"Right up there," he said, "at the top of the hill. It is right on top of us. There use to be a road. That's how Grant got up there. Maybe that road is still there. I ain't ben up here on this piece of river for thirty year."

"I blieve I will try out some of that pink slab cake," I said.

"Don't do me no favors," said the cook.

With the war on there was a terrible shortage of pilots and the companies were really out shaking the bushes. This old pilot had gone off booming in 1889, knocked around on the Ohio, the Cumberland, the Big Sandy, and down on the Ouachita, wandered up the Missouri, got married in Great Falls, wandered off again to the Columbia, drifted north and ended up a pilot on the Great Slave Lake in the Northwest Territory north of Alberta.

"What's it like up there?" I asked him and I expected a little James Oliver Curwood stuff but that's not the way it works.

"Hot as hell in summer and colder than Kelly's ice house in winter," that's all he said, except that the mosquitoes would steal your hat.

He had been retired for fifteen years when the war came along and they rousted him out. He wasn't very happy about it. His niece that he lived with, her and her husband, spilled the beans and told somebody he was a retired steamboat pilot. Everybody on the river thought he was dead or in Hudson's Bay or some such place. Because he wasn't the kind that sends a 25-for-$1.59 Christmas card to the *Waterways Journal* every year saying, "This year I have been a subscriber for 48 years. In August I had a fine trip to Mammoth Cave with my niece and her husband and the kiddies. Best wishes to all the crew."

So before long they came. I don't know who "they" are exactly, but "they" are always showing up, and they told him it was his patriotic duty to go back to piloting. So here he was, and he had to have me or a deckhand in the pilot house at night to hunt buoys for him with the searchlight and field glasses. He eventually knocked the stacks down on the bridge over Kentucky Dam.

I finished my slab cake and went out on the tow and checked our tie-off lines and our four lonesome barges full of golden grain all the way from the northern prairies west of Fargo. They were just laying there without a word to say, far from home. The fireman was setting in a chair on deck by the fire room.

"*This* fog ain't agoing to lift," he said.

"I'm going up the hill," I said.

"Now what I'd like to find me," he said, "is a nice little two-handful widow with some green in the sugar bowl."

There was not much to see up there in the battlefield in the dark. There is the usual cannonball stuck in an oak tree, I suppose, but that tree would be getting along now if it were big enough to stop a cannonball in 1862. I looked down on the river from up there, swatting mosquitoes, and tried to imagine what it was like back then, with the federal boats tied up right down below, right exactly where we were laying. Through the foggy mist I could see the fireman sitting on the guard, he hadn't moved a muscle and was still dreaming about that little widow, which is, if you think about it, what practically everybody wanted. Even the married men would have liked to have a nice plump little widow on the side with some green in the sugar bowl.

Steamboating with Central Barge was full of surprises. You never knew where they would send you next. Here I was way down in Tennessee amongst the kudzu and peanuts, on one of those history-book battlefields from that romantic war of long ago they write so many books about. And now people came to eat baloney sandwiches and snap pickles where exactly 80 years before to the month "the rebel dead lay in winrows and both our dead and the rebels lay in every direction." Somewhere here in the gloom were the Peach Orchard, the Hornets' Nest, and Bloody Pond. A victory for General Grant, peacetime misfit from Galena, Illinois, home port of the *Grey Eagle*, most famous packet on the Upper Mississippi. After Grant left town with the Twenty-first Illinois Volunteers, the *Grey Eagle* hit the Rock Island bridge, a total loss, and her owner Captain Daniel Smith Harris, most widely known of the hundred captains then working on the Upper Mississippi, retired "heartbroken" from the river he had almost personally invented in 1823. And to add insult to ignominy, part of the bottom and side planks of the *Grey Eagle* were used for years afterwards as board sidewalks in Rock Island.

Things tie together. Mark Twain's publishing house, Charles L. Webster and Company, later published the dying Grant's *Memoirs*, which earned about a half-a-million dollars for the war hero's widow. Grant in his innocence had expected to make maybe ten thousand dollars on the effort. And effort it was. He was dead broke and dying of cancer of the throat.

In 1885 when he was riding high with the Grant book, Mark Twain danced up and down and crowed, "It seems that everything I touch turns to gold." But nine years later, on the brink of financial disaster, he was in another one of his moods of black despondency and referred to the Grant bonanza as "that terrible book" which had lured him into false expectations and bankruptcy. "Mark Twain was a devil to do business with," as his great nephew Samuel Charles

Webster said. Mark Twain used Samuel Webster's father, Charles L. Webster, as scapegoat in the bustup. "Mark Twain never forgave anyone he had injured," as the younger Webster noted.

But now it was many many years later and perhaps it didn't matter any more; Mark Twain was as dead as the soldiers here on the hill in their graves, the United States had had several more splendid wars, and was in a good one right then. And lots of new and improved ways of killing people had been thought up.

I walked back down the little road to the landing and the boat. The boys on watch had left the galley and were sitting around on the forward deck and the stern of the barges. They were talking. There are practically no silent men on a steamboat and *no* silent Southerners.

Most of us on the boat were from Illinois and Iowa and Wisconsin and Minnesota, but the deckhands and the cook were from Guntersville, Alabama, and sitting around in the cool of the evening we had to fight the Civil War over again. The Southern boys didn't know much about it but they fought it over anyway. They dealt in warmed-over cabbage mostly.

"That General Grant was a rumpot," one of them would say.

"If he was, Lee should of got aholt of some of his brand," says the fireman.

"At Bull Run the Yanks throwed down their guns and run for home," says a deckhand named Malvern Murch.

"Well youse done lost the war," says the fireman. "If youse would of ben men enough you'd a done the whippin instead of gettin whipped."

"Malvern go check that steam siphon in the fuel flat," I

said and away he went, rising on the balls of his feet, and pretty soon we could hear him cussing that steam siphon.

"Garters," says the other deckhand from Guntersville out of the blue. "I was in a cat house one time in Mobile and there's four girls cool as you please setting there listening to Little Jack Little on the radio without a stitch on but them high silk stockings and garters."

"I seen Little Jack Little in person one time," says the mess boy. "In Memphis, Tennessee."

The fog lifted a little so our old, old captain decided he had better make some kind of an effort. Try to make a showing.

"Turn her loose," he said, "and we'll give her a try."

The deckhands went off grumbling.

So we turned loose and started up the Tennessee River again. In a couple of hours we came up to Pickwick Dam and we locked through and headed up into the pool. That's what they call the lake above a dam — the pool.

The steamboat is sighing and panting and chow-chowing her way along and nobody is paying us much attention. Up ahead the channel lights are winking at us. You think of a steamboat as being quiet but an old timer like this working full throttle gasped and roared, quivered and struggled. We used to hear the old *Muscatine* and the *Mildred* coming a mile away. After they lay me away I will still hear that wonderful sound, and my smeller will still smell escaping steam, scorching oil, and soft-coal gas.

When I went with Central Barge I told Captain A. C. Ingersoll, Jr., I wanted to go into the engine room. I had been reading William McFee.

"Don't be a damn fool," he said. "There's no glory in the engine room!"

"No," I said, "but the engineers don't freeze to death in the winter either."

I went on deck of course. He took an interest in me, and I looked up to him. And that's why I have this moustache to-day. Because Connie Ingersoll had one. That's the first thing I set to work on when I went with Central — growing a moustache. It looked real fine around the bars of Alton and St. Louis and St. Paul. Connie Ingersoll was a daredevil and years later he drowned crossing Green Bay, in Lake Michigan, in a small sailboat. When you get to be my age you don't hardly dare pick up the *Waterways Journal** anymore. Every week it seems another old buddy from the river leaves for that big pilot house or that big engine room or that big bunk room in the sky.

Mark Twain did not wear a moustache when he was piloting. There is an "original oil portrait" of him owned by the Keokuk Public Library, supposed to be from "about 1859." He was piloting then but he has no moustache in this picture, only sort of mutton-chop sideburns. There is another picture, a photograph labeled "about the time he quit the river," and the mutton chops are gone and he's sporting a pencil-thin Clark Gable model moustache. Same in Virginia City in 1863. When he went to San Francisco in 1864 he let himself go in the bristle department and the famous Mark Twain full-droop moustache was born.

Now from where we were sitting out on the barges we could see the red and the green running lights up beside the stacks.

This steamboat was built for Doctor Will Mayo of the Mayo brothers of Rochester, Minnesota. He was so blame

---

* The *Waterways Journal*, the "Riverman's Bible," has been published weekly at St. Louis since 1887. The address is 721 Olive Street, the subscription $7.50 per annum payable in gold, scrip, turnips, or baled hay.

rich he could afford to have a full-size sternwheel steamboat built just for a pleasure boat. But one time they were laying at a landing someplace, it must have been during the Depression, and there was a bunch of men standing around on the bank gawping, down and out and no jobs, no prospects, and families to feed, and Dr. Will's conscience got to him and he sold the boat, he said it wasn't right for him to live like that when so many people had nothing.

Then it went to the Corps of Engineers at Fountain City, Wisconsin, and it was called the *General Allen* and it shoved barges for channel work and rip-rap. Finally it went up for auction and Central Barge was hard up for towboats with the war on so they bought her and gave her back her original name: *Minnesota*. She was not intended to handle heavy barges and we pulled all the cavels off the foredeck when we made up tow in Paducah.

The steamboats are nearly all gone. It all happened so fast, like the trolleys, like the passenger pigeons, and the passenger trains. At one time you could go from Baltimore, Maryland, to Brunswick, Maine, by trolley car. William Ellery Channing, the great historian, said the trolley car was the greatest invention of mankind because it gave so many people so much pleasure. Then along came Henry Ford and busted up that theory and made us what we are today. All the older men on the river now — I mean men of fifty-five or sixty — started on steamboats. I started decking on the steamer *James W. Good* of the Federal Barge Line, and later on I was third deckhand and second cook on the giant sternwheeler *Alexander Mackenzie*. I have personally steamboated with old scrawny deckhands out of the Pittsburgh pools from the days when they had no bunk rooms, they laid down where they could. And they pumped bilge out of those Consolidation coal boats with spring-pole pumps.

Working and living on a real steamboat was a lot different from life on a diesel boat, no matter how big. A Western river steamboat on a long run carried a barge alongside full of coal called a "fuel flat." To make the boat go the deckhands wheeled the coal out of the fuel flat in wheelbarrows and they dumped it in the fire room. The fireman built a fire under the boilers and made steam and the steam made the boat go. On a steamboat everybody was aware of the engines and the boilers and the fires and the coal. But on a diesel boat there is not much of a to-do. To fuel up you stick a hose in a hole in the deck and that's that. The engines are pretty boring because there are usually no moving parts visible and they don't smell right. Oh, I like *all* engine rooms but there is a big difference between steam and diesel believe me. A steamboat almost seems alive.

Captain Marryat was on a steamboat, way back in 1838 on the Upper Mississippi above Galena, "the present emporium of the Mineral Country," and he wrote in his journal: "It is this appearance of breathing which makes the high pressure (steam) engine the nearest approach to creation which was ever attained by the ingenuity of man."

And of steamboating on the Ohio in 1823 Giacomo Beltrami, the Henry Armetta of nineteenth-century travel writers, observed: "The passengers are provided with . . beds, to which the noise of the water and the machinery imparts a soporific virtue not to be found elsewhere."

Mark Twain never became enthralled by the engine room. Perhaps it was beneath him in more ways than its physical location. At any rate the magic seductions of crossheads and rocker arms and doctor pumps never reached him. Some people were afraid of steamboat engines and their ways and liked to stay away from them. They were mysterious creatures and best left to the engineers.

George Byron Merrick, on the other hand, gives equal billing to the engineers, and devotes two chapters to their art and their spirit: "Courageous, proud of their calling, and to be depended upon to do their duty under any and all circumstances; giving, if need be, their lives for the safety of the passengers and crew of the boat." His particular idols were George McDonald and Billy Hamilton. Merrick is unusual in that in his career on the river he filled positions not only as steersman and pilot, but also as clerk and cub engineer. He says he would have become a capable engineer except that "Scaling boilers decided me not to persevere in the engineering line."

We usually reached Galena Thursday evening. As soon as the boat was made fast the "mud-valves" were opened, the fires drawn, the water let out of the boilers, and the process of cleaning began. Being a slim lad, one of my duties was to creep into the boilers through the manhole, which was just large enough to let me through. . . . To lie flat on one's stomach on the top of a twelve inch flue, studded with rivet heads, with a space of only fifteen inches above one's head, and in this position haul a chain back and forth without any leverage whatever, simply by the muscles of the arm, with the thermometer 90° in the shade, was a practice well calculated to disillusionize anyone not wholly given over to mechanics. While I liked mechanics I knew when I had enough, and therefore reached out for something one deck higher. The unexpected disability of our "mud" clerk, as the second clerk is called on the river, opened the way for an ascent, and I promptly availed myself of it.

"Now you take your Pittsburgh," said the striker engineer. "Them Mellons all come from Pittsburgh but are not interested in the Monongahela or the Allegheny not a one of them ever took no interest in none of their own steamboats they never even rode on one much lest gettin into the engine room and gettin a license."

"The Mellons don't have no steamboats," I said. "They are bankers."

"They got their finger in everything," says the striker. "Don't tell me they don't own no steamboats. I bet they own fifty steamboats if the truth was known. Anyway they got to sit in an office all day while we are going up and down the river. Don't make good sense to me."

The conversation rolled on and on in rhythm with the pitmans, which were laboriously cranking us up the river.

"So the farmer's wife says 'I already did, but now he wants me to give him a chicken.' "

"Why that redhead was as independent as a hog on ice. I never got nuthin offa her."

"Maybe you ain't the man you use to be, Slim, maybe you better lay holt of some of them there veetamine pills."

"So the guy says to her, 'No, but you are breakin my glasses.' "

"I heard that one different. I heard . . ."

"She busted her shaft right above Genoa lock. If you think we wasn't goin round and around there for a while. Finely got a line onto a stump. That night Shorty smuggled a bottle aboard and . . ."

"Why hell man down in my home town they is dozens of em hangin around in the taverns just awaitin for it. Smart lookin gals too, some of em."

"And teacher says 'Johnny, what do you mean, Johnny?' and the kid says 'Oh teacher I heard him say, "Pull down the curtain and . . ." ' "

"So we got a pint of booze and went back and started throwin rocks at the house. The old hoor she come out with a shotgun . . ."

"If you wanna shove somethin, try this, says the brunette . . ."

Crude, coarse, rough, rattle-brained, foolish, we were all those; and repetitive, boastful, vulgar, rank, pugnacious, and often pitiful. Hamlin Garland went to the Yukon in the gold rush to mingle with the brave prospectors and observe their nobility at close hand. He had a rude shock and found his companions men who "were filthy and profane and made enjoyment of nature impossible." He became "worn out with the filth and foolishness of many of these men." He said that they had "nothing of the epic qualities," and that they were "men to whom drink was a luxury and vice an entertainment."

We weren't that bad but none of us was up for Sunday School superintendent either. Rivermen were considered a bad lot, but we weren't all ruffians, although we had a murderer in our midst. We had standards. A man who abused women and children and dogs was despised. Drugs had not become a national pastime, and a "dope fiend" was at the bottom of the garbage pail. "Going on the river" had its own special implications.

My mother had been reared in an Ohio River town and had a firsthand knowledge of the character of rivermen as a group. She knew three daughters of a prominent river captain who were about her own age: these daughters could swear a hole through a brick fence and the young ladies from respectable families in town were not allowed to play with them. Rivermen, by and large, had a reputation for coarse living. My mother did not care to see her son fall into this pithole of iniquity.*

* This is from *Pilotin' Comes Natural* by Frederick Way Jr. A witty and charming book.

Drinking, swearing, fighting, thieving, gambling, and whoring have always been treated as "colorful" and "romantic frontier" aspects of the river, especially by Mark Twain.* The profanity of the mate is always dwelt upon lovingly. It was "funny."

As for drink, all his life Mark Twain himself was an enthusiastic guzzler of hot scotches, champagne, cocktails, blue-blazers, slings, juleps, cobblers, claret cups, Ramos gin fizzes, Sazerac, Roman punch, Baltimore eggnogs, and Sangaree. Pap Finn was a roaring drunk, the Shepherdsons drank, there was a bar on every boat, and the bar of the Planters' House in St. Louis was *the* meeting place, for steamboat men and all other lordly characters. The King and the Duke tie one on aboard the raft. And when Jim gets bitten by the snake he takes to the ever-present whiskey jug and gets roaring drunk. No wonder this book got lambasted on publication and was immediately banned in Concord, Massachusetts, and scorned publicly by such as Louisa May Alcott.

And for the rest of it, I was raised among boys in a small Mississippi River town and I know what Tom and Huck and Joe Harper talked about and it was not entirely about "goin fishin" and "playin hookey." And when we come to those rotten bums in *Huckleberry Finn*, the King and the Duke, their actual conversations on the raft probably would make the modern practitioners of literary smut seem like *Ruth Fielding at Sunrise Farm*.

I took a stroll out to the head of the tow with Lee Roy the deckhand. We sat down and listened to the barges gurgling.

---

* Well, not whoring. He handled this omnipresent feature of the nineteenth and other centuries by ignoring it.

"See anything up there in that battlefield?" he said.

"No," I said. "It was too dark."

"Was that there a good one for our side?"

"No, you got beat. It was about a dead heat but the history books say we beat. Twenty thousand dead, Lee Roy."

"Jesus Christ."

We sat for a while and looked at the channel lights ahead.

"Listen, how come you aren't in the Army?" I said.

"I get mad when you holler at me, and I get mad when Cap chews me out. But if I get mad enough here I can quit. You can't quit that there Army. Besides, I ain't interested in killin nobody."

"You got a wrong attitude," I said. "What if everybody thought like that?"

"Why then nobody would go and there wouldn't be no war."

"Gimme the makins," I said. "I'm out."

"You figger they'll have them pig irons loaded when we get up here to Sheffield?"

"Don't know yet."

"I ain't fond of them loads of pig irons."

Mark Twain was in the Confederate Army for two weeks at which point he "resigned," explaining that he was "incapacitated by fatigue through persistent retreating." And although he was by nature a champion guilt-seeker, this defection was not on his list of personal horrors. He lit out for the Territory by overland stage to Nevada and that was the end of the War Between the States for him. And it was also his farewell to piloting and the Mississippi River. It was July, 1861.

There is no record of little Jean, Susy, or Clara Clemens ever coming to their father and saying in plaintive tones, "Papa, what did *you* do in the Great War?"

Lee Roy and I, we got off the war and smoked for a while and we talked about women. About the girls we had had, and ones we wished we had had, and ones we were going to have pretty soon, most any time now.

General Grant lost 13,673 men at Shiloh. The rebs lost 14,687 and their general was killed, General Albert S. Johnston. Grant beat, and proceeded to Corinth, Mississippi, which he captured one month later.

We finally got to Sheffield, Alabama, and, sure enough, there were four loads of pig iron waiting for us to take down the Tennessee to the Ohio and up past Golconda and Rosiclare, Caseyville, and Shawneetown — all the way to Evansville.

The old pilot blew a nice long mournful landing whistle just to let everybody know the old *Minnesota* had arrived safe and sound in Alabama.

NINE

Enter the Lawyers with
Their Pointy Teeth

In describing a pilot's life and work on the Mississippi
Mark Twain dredged up all the horrors of that trade he
could remember and he did a good job. For a compulsive
prevaricator* he pretty much stuck to the facts for once, and
the facts of life on the old lower river included a constantly
shifting channel, no aids to navigation, no U.S. Corps of
Engineers dredging projects; a river immensely wide, fast
flowing, with an appalling volume of flow per minute; a river
alternately in flood and in precarious low water stages; and
a river invisibly filled with ferocious snags, stumps, blind
reefs, bluff reefs, creeping sandbars, and sunken wrecks,
which "could snatch the hull timbers" from under a steamboat and "destroy a quarter of a million dollars worth of
steamboat and cargo in five minutes."

Horrors were as popular then as now, and everybody doted
on steamboat explosions, train wrecks, shipwrecks, tidal
waves, fires, orphanage volcanic eruptions providing there
were enough casualties, death-dealing earthquakes, and other

---

* Charlie Webster, Mark Twain's great nephew, on the subject of his
famous uncle's autobiography: "It was at this period that he started
out to tell the truth and made an awful botch of it. He shouldn't have
tried it so late in life."

disasters. So he had something to work on, and he enjoyed it. But one navigational hazard that has driven pilots of the Upper Mississippi crazy for generations is *bridges*. And they didn't *have* any bridges on the Lower Mississippi. They didn't even have Eads bridge at St. Louis until 1874. And by that time Mark was living in Hartford and hobnobbing with the eastern literati and building a house on Farmington Avenue which had more extras to it than a Lady Baltimore cake.

Pilots, captains, and owners of steamboats and towboats have been at war with the bridges of the Upper Mississippi (and also those of the Ohio, the Illinois, the Monongahela and all the other navigable rivers) ever since the first bridge was built at Rock Island in 1856. There are two kinds of bridges up here. The railroad bridges have a swing span that pivots on a limestone pier leaving two openings in the bridge with that nasty pier in the middle and one on each side.* The other kind of bridge is a "high bridge," the height being great enough to allow even big boats like the packet boat *Delta Queen* to pass under without knocking down the stacks or "chimbleys." High bridges were originally called "wagon bridges." Now they carry a constant stream of autos, Air-Stream trailers and long-haul giant semis. But my mother who is ninety-three years of age still calls the Eagle Point high bridge the "wagon bridge," just like a lot of people call Dubuque harbor the "ice harbor" because 8,000,000 years ago like back in 1895 and 1917 the steamboats used to lay up for the winter in there as a harbor of refuge so they would not get cut down when the river ice moved out in the spring. High bridges have the bridge piers far apart and are supposed to be easy to run and no trouble. The channel span

---

* There is one lift bridge on the Upper Mississippi — at Keithsburg, Illinois. The whole span rises up in the air on cables, slowly, slowly. It has real style.

of the new highway bridge at Dubuque is 355 feet wide. However, due to wind, current, rudder trouble, engine failure, or the mysteries of fate, towboats nowadays with tremendous power and magnificent steering systems manage sometimes to hit the piers, bust up the tow and fill the river with runaway or sunken barges, or even to sink the towboat itself. The most tragic event of this kind in recent years was when the big towboat *Natchez* hit the pier of the Greenville, Mississippi, highway bridge, which has a span of no less than 800 feet, sinking the boat and killing fourteen of the crew. The boat has never even been located, much less raised.

Ridiculous! What's the matter with these guys? Some rotten piloting!

No, pardner, it's just the damn Mississippi River.

The old Hastings, Minnesota, bridge had a horizontal clearance of 106 feet. A barge tow three barges wide is 105 feet wide. So we used to go down from St. Paul two barges wide, 70 feet, giving a clearance of 36 feet. In spite of excessive care, sweat, skill, and prayers, this bridge took a continual beating over the years and was the direct cause of over two billion cubic feet of pilot house hot air, cussing, threats and vilifications, all directed at an inanimate object made of steel and rivets.

We were up at the saloon near the Smith Avenue highway bridge waiting for empty barges one time and the pilot was sitting there hanging onto a Grain Belt beer and looking pretty morose.

"What's the matter, Cap?" I said. "Didn't you get no letter from that old girl in Alton?"

"I don't know," he said. "Somehow it just don't seem right. I got that god damn, ———, ———, ———, Hastings bridge the last three trips down. They'll be finished unloading up there at Northern States in a couple of hours and when I go on watch we'll be at Pig's Eye or Pine Bend and I'll get the _____, _____, _____, _____, _____, _____ Hastings bridge *again*."

(NOTE: I am so old fashioned I don't like to see these words in print. Mark Twain put a lot of fancy cussing in *Huckleberry Finn* and *Life on the Mississippi* but it was all vaudeville stuff, suitable for a Chautauqua reading. It was "funny." Real swearing on the river is effective but not funny usually, and tends to be repetitive and eventually wearisome. The only stimulating and inventive swearing I ever heard on the river was from Southerners. They have a way of being atrociously profane and funny at the same time.)

The finest crack pilot I ever worked for as mate on the upper river (what Mark Twain called a "lightning pilot") eventually hit the Hastings bridge, knocked the drawbridge off its underpinnings, and put the bridge out of commission for two weeks.

Coming upstream with 15,000 tons of Illinois coal, the mammoth sternwheeler *Alexander Mackenzie* caught a notch in the center pier of the Burlington Railroad drawbridge at Burlington, Iowa, and knocked the bullnosing and a few tons of limestone blocks as big as piano cases off, and continued walking up the river without the slightest pause. This is a case of 15,000 tons of coal meeting an immovable object. In this case the immovable object decided to move.

Waterways Journal, July 1, 1972.

DELTA QUEEN IS INVOLVED IN ACCIDENT
AT MADISON, IND.

The Greene Line steamer *Delta Queen* was involved in an accident at Madison, Ind., June 28, about 11:40 PM when fog suddenly closed down as she started through the Madison highway bridge. The port side of the *Queen* scraped one of the piers, doing some damage to the railings, rub strips on the hull, etc. However after a Coast Guard inspection, the boat was allowed to proceed into Louisville, where repairs were to be made by Jeffboat, Inc. personnel. . . . After hitting the pier the *Queen* reportedly angled into and damaged some docking craft and damaged some docking floats for pleasure craft. The Ohio River was high and the current through the bridge swift at the time of the mishap.

Enter the lawyers with their pointy teeth, beady eyes and briefcases. Now the owners of the docking floats will sue the *Queen*, the *Queen* will sue the bridge, the bridge will sue the *Queen* right back, and a lady passenger from Napoleon, Ohio, will sue the Greene Line for damage to her nerves. Nobody will get anything out of it except the lawyers, who will spend three weeks at Key Biscayne the following February.

Most of the railroad swing bridges on the western waters were built in the nineteenth century, and, although commercial boating conditions have changed, the bridges have not. They remain exactly as they were in the days of the kerosene lamp and the parlor stove, and twice as exasperating. And dangerous to shipping. Here's when some typical railroad bridges on the Upper Mississippi first reared their black skeletons across the virgin stream:

Winona, Minn., 1870 (Chicago Northwestern)
La Crosse, Wis., 1877 (Chicago Milwaukee St. P. & P.)
Dubuque, Iowa, 1868 (Illinois Central)
Sabula, Ill., 1881 (C.M. St. P. & P.)
Davenport, Iowa, 1872 (Chicago Rock Island)
Keokuk, Iowa, 1871 (Wabash & Toledo)

Quincy, Ill., 1867 (C.B. & Q.)
Hannibal, Mo., 1868 (Wabash)

It is just as bad or worse on other rivers and the conditions on the Illinois River send Don Grot, an editor on the *Waterways Journal*, right up the lock wall.

The bridge situation along the Illinois, as on most other waterways, is sheer frustration for towboat pilots. In all, there are twelve bridges on the Illinois that cause continual problems, because of bad locations or inadequate clearances, for barge line navigation. Ten of these bridges belong to various railroads and remain unimproved year after year.*

Imagine for a moment a tow over 1,000 feet long and 105 feet wide trying to negotiate the Chicago, Burlington and Quincy Railroad Bridge at Beardstown, which was built on a sharp bend. The problem is compounded by the fact the bridge provides only 118 feet of horizontal clearance: a mere margin of 13 feet for possible error.

Right on, there, Don. And remember folks, a string of barges that size could be carrying as much as 18,000 tons or more. You can't stop that on a dime or maneuver it like putting your car in the garage. Oh it's hell, boys, but Mother always said there would be days like this. But she never said they was going to come like bananas, in bunches. And she never said nothing about bridges.

Five hundred years before the birth of Christ, King Xerxes of Persia led his soldiers across the Hellespont on a pontoon bridge. Two thousand three hundred and eighty years later the engineers of the Chicago, Milwaukee, St. Paul

---

* The "media" (won't that word *ever* go away?) don't know it but Vietnam was not the longest war in our history, the *Waterways Journal* has been in pitched battle with the railroads since 1887. That's 86 years. And they just brought up some new artillery last week.

and Pacific Railroad threw two pontoon bridges across the Mississippi, one at Reads Landing, Minnesota, and one at Marquette, Iowa. Mark Twain passed through both of these two steam-operated curiosities, one at page 572 in *Life on the Mississippi* and the other at page 576, but he mentions neither. Matter of fact he noticed practically nothing of interest on this trip, was probably too busy talking to notice. Too bad. They would have appealed to his life-long interest in Rube Goldberg contraptions. On the other hand it's just as well. If he had seen them he'd have tried to buy the patent on the idea and told poor old Charley Webster to add pontoon bridges to the line and get out and hustle up some live accounts. But he could have got some fun in the book out of describing their eccentric bridge behavior, instead of which he came up with such stimulating stuff as "La Crosse is a town of twelve or thirteen thousand population, with electric lighted streets, and with blocks of buildings which are stately enough . . . to command respect in any city."

The first edition of *Life on the Mississippi* weighs 2 lbs. 12 oz. and about 1½ lbs. of it has the same gripping and poetic literary quality as this information about the electric streetlights of La Crosse.

These floating bridges have been abandoned and removed entirely, but not until recent years, and I have been through them both many many times and never failed to marvel at the fact that they actually worked. I have even been through the one at Marquette on a *raft*, how do you like them onions Mr. Clemens?

The main idea is that when a boat blows for the draw to open, the bridge-tender lets go one side of the pontoon draw span and the current pushes it down so it is hanging parallel to the shore. The boat, or the boat and string of barges, passes through and then the bridge-tender pulls the pontoon span back into place with a donkey engine. How does he do that? There's a chain from the donkey engine to the lower end of the pontoon span that falls down and lies on the bottom of the river while the boat passes through. Well that'll give you an idea except for the really goofy part, which is that the level of the river is forever rising and falling which means the level of the pontoon railroad track has to be constantly adjusted to stay on the same plane with the fixed track on the rest of the bridge — which requires jacks, brummits, frambolts, bargles, arfblocks, whingles, etc. The idea that both these bridges survived ice, floods, steamboats, log rafts, and their own idiosyncrasies for over 80 years, and without ever sending the bridge-tenders to the funny farm, always seemed incredible to the idle bystander; but this was before the days of Welfare so there were hardly ever any idle bystanders to wonder about it.

Both these freaks are now gone but practically all the other ancient railroad bridges of the Upper Mississippi remain, to the background music, *fortissimo*, of maledictions by the members high and low of the river fraternity. This puts me personally in a rather awkward position because I am a dedicated railroad fan* as well as a sandbar-silly votary of the river in all its meanings. But I don't have to run through these bridges, run them with eighteen empty jumbo barges in a November gale with a four-story derrick barge on the hip — so they don't bother me any more. They strike me as baroque, fanciful, beautiful in their steely realism, even poetic.

Mark Twain's only mention that I recall of a railroad

* Mark Twain was the only licensed Mississippi River pilot ever to live in an Italian palace as his home, but I am the only licensed Mississippi River pilot ever to have ridden in the locomotive cab of the Guayaquil and Quito railroad while negotiating the hair-raising "Devil's Nose" switchback in the mountains of Ecuador.

bridge is in *Life on the Mississippi*. Again, it was part of the chronicle of that deadly dull trip from St. Louis to St. Paul in 1882. They came up to Louisiana, Missouri, before dawn.

"There was a railway bridge here well sprinkled with glowing lights, and a very beautiful sight it was."

No doubt. But you see he didn't have to run it, either. He was retired from the noble profession. He was a passenger. A storm in the Rockies with plenty of lightning is beautiful to behold if you are not an airplane pilot trying to get through it, and as long as you don't have to mess around with a bridge it can be a rhapsody.

Bridges *are* romantic. London Bridge, Tower Bridge, Waterloo Bridge start the drums of history rolling and the heart keeping time. Then there's old Haji Abdu and his regretful meetings on the "bridge of Time," and Horatius at the Bridge, and Lord Byron:

> *I stood in Venice on the Bridge of Sighs,*
> *A palace and a prison on each hand.*

(Mark Twain marched across the Bridge of Sighs in the *Innocents Abroad* but it brought forth no poetry; only when he got to the dungeons and tortures at the other end of the bridge did his pen catch fire. Delicious horrors! Awful ones: thumb screws, head crushers, water tortures — lovely! Right up his alley. Worse luck, though. No ghosts. Give Mark a ghost, even a small-time, two-bit ghost and he was good for four or five pages at least.)

There's Remagen Bridge — Caesar's bridge across the Rhine constructed entirely of irregular Latin verbs — The Bridge of San Luis Rey and its erudite bridge-tender Thorny Wilder — the Rockdale Viadock — and Ambrose Bierce's "Incident at Owl Creek Bridge," which brings us back to the Tennessee River by mistake. That was another railroad bridge, the kind the Masters Mates and Pilots Association don't like.

How did the railroads get the upper hand against the brave captains and the true-blue steamboat owners who had opened the West and contributed all that love and color? Well it happened in 1857 and it was too bad. It was like this.

On May 6, 1856, the pilot of the steamboat *Effie Afton* made a mistake, a big history-making mistake like Napoleon deciding to move ahead into Moscow instead of going home to a warm supper. What he did was, he hit the brand new railroad bridge across the Mississippi at Rock Island, Illinois. The *Effie* — shocked — burned and sank a total loss.

After thinking this over for a whole year the owners of the deceased steamboat decided to sue the bridge, claiming it was an obstruction to navigation. So they filed suit in the U.S. District Court in Chicago and everybody packed box lunches and gathered for a good fight.

History doesn't let anybody know what's going on until it is all over. If everybody knew they were making history they would get all self-conscious and blush like anything. What everybody *thought* was happening in this case was just a damage suit. But here's what was going on, and the dreadful result. Benjamin P. Thomas knows and here's what he says:

The case had significance far beyond the property loss involved — it was a conflict of sections, economies, and eras. It arrayed the east-west railroad axis against the north-south river axis; New Orleans and St. Louis against the new era of railroads. And it involved highly technical problems of mechanical engineering, bridge construction, river currents, and navigation. After listening to two weeks of testimony and four days of argument by counsel, the jury disagreed — a virtual victory for the railroad interests.

Virtual victory indeed! A crusher, and a ruinous calamity for the *Effie Afton* and all her contemporaries and all steamboats, gas boats, naptha launches, excursion boats, dredge boats, house boats, john boats, show boats, sand barges, log rafts, diesel towboats, canoes — all the boats that were to follow, right up to the present time and the sextuple screw 25,000 horsepower new mammoth kort-nozzled, chromium-galleyed, wall-to-wall-air-conditioned diesel towboat *Charles T. Repulsive*, launched only last week.

Now whose fault was this? Why of course, the wily lawyer for the Rock Island Bridge, a sinister Bad Man in a swallow tail coat and a black hat.

But wait! What was this shyster's name? A name to be forever recorded by rivermen in infamy?

In the words of Tex Ritter:

". . . and his name was

Abe-ra-ham Lin-coln."

TEN

Sure Was Pretty Back in Them Days

Al and I read *Huckleberry Finn* and we took it seriously. Not the blood and thunder and the murders and the tar and featherings and the farce and movie serial melodrama — we got plenty of that every Saturday at the Princess and the Dreamland for 15 cents with a half a pound of peanut-butter kisses for another dime. It was the rafting. Floating down the river on a raft, accountable to nobody, *that* was the point. We had Mycroft's copy, in the Uniform Edition, Red Cloth, Crown 8vo, which Aunt Sue Pike had given him on his thirteenth birthday, January 11, 1923, With Love from Aunt Sue, and we took turns on it and marked passages and drew maps, made lists ("frying pan, watertight coffee can for matches, hunting knife, peanut butter . . .") and we passed notes about it in Algebra class. We were just kidding ourselves of course. None of the guys did things like that. They played ball and made crystal sets out of oatmeal boxes and went on overnight hikes to Palmer's Creek. It looked pretty hopeless.

We were sixteen years old and we brooded about that raft trip and talked about it and talked about it and summer vacation came. Summers in Iowa were long, hot and lovely. Lemonade pitchers tinkled among the wicker furniture and palm leaf fans on my grandfather's shady porch. Mr. Kopple's horse plodded around the hill district drawing the ice-cream wagon. We were always taking our clothes off to go swimming or putting them on after swimming. We swam at Rocky Bottom, Muddy Bottom, Newtons, Number 16 Bridge, Swallow Bank, Cascade Crossing — all in Catfish Creek. Wherever there was a puddle we took off our clothes instantly and jumped in. We also swam in the Mississippi at Eagle Point, at Lefty Shuster's, Steamboat Hollow, Lake Peosta, the Harbor, Pearl Island, and on various sandbars. We jumped out of the rowboat and swam in the channel in the big rollers behind the infrequent steamboats. We also squirted each other with garden hoses and dumped pails of water on each other.

The heat pressed in from all sides. There was no such thing as air conditioning or even attic insulation. Houses became "bake ovens." We lay down in heat and woke up in flames. The sun bore down on Iowa, Illinois, Nebraska, Kansas. "It's good for the corn," everybody said. "Good corn weather." People who hadn't the remotest emotional or financial connection with "the corn" said it over and over, same as they said: "Well it's your *dry* cold, anyway," when the temperature went to thirty below in January.

In the evenings "heat lightning" quivered on the horizon. Thunderstorms wandered up from Bellevue, doused the town ("Hurry up and close the attic windows Richard!"), yawed off to Cuba City ("I guess it's over. Richard, go up and open the attic windows again"), and returned via Spechts Ferry to cannonade and drench us again ("Fred, you better go up and close the attic windows").

Every so often a horrendous electrical storm would rake the area, splitting asunder two-hundred-year-old oaks, setting barns on fire, and terrifying everyone. After the storm it would get hotter.

We consumed huge amounts of water, ice chips, root beer, lemonade, Green River, Cosley's white soda, cream soda, strawberry soda, Nehi, Whistle, and Blatz's grape soda.

We decided the only correct thing to do about that raft trip was to run away. In the words of Tom Sawyer, page 306 of *Huckleberry*, it would be "the *right* way — and the regular way. . . . And there ain't no *other* way, *I* ever heard of." We would run away — kids were constantly running away from home in all the books — and it would be gaudy, bully, and all those other things and would cause a tremendous effect, not only among the other guys, but with Billie Jane, Phyllis, Evvie, and Marjorie. We would bum our way north, build a raft on an island, and float down to Dubuque. *That* would make a few people such as civics teachers sit up and take notice. Real American boys with adventure in their blood, honest-to-God river rats with plenty of grit.

"Oh there wasn't much to it. We just bummed the freights to Winona and . . ."

"Geez, you really bum the freights?"

"Sure. It's the only way to *get* someplace. Then we swiped an axe out of this old cabin and we cut down these six cottonwood trees on this old island across from Red Wing and built ourselves a good old raft . . ."

But I guess we knew we wouldn't run away. Every once in a while I would gaze through the pink clouds of euphoria and see my father reading my "Running Away" note and the results were not good. My old man would not chuckle and say "A chip off the old block" or "Don't worry, Mother, that boy has real sand." No, he would call out the police, the Pinkertons and the Governor's Greys and I would be back at the old homestead in twenty-four hours confined to bar-racks and my mother would be wearing her Patient Resignation face.

I was working in stock picking orders down at "Glovers" that summer. John Blades and I were picking sheep-lined coats, Brown's Beach Jackets, leather coats, and winter underwear on the fifth floor, with a good view of the river at the east end. Al was working at a drug store, and behind the scenes at a drug store he learned a lot — the dreary facts about secret miseries, frightened girls, bleak malfunctions by the score.

One blistering afternoon I went down in the elevator, went into Father's office, closed the door and said "Dad, Al and I are going up to Winona and make a raft and float down to Dubuque."

Till the day he died I never could tell how my old man was going to react to anything.

"Your mother is not going to like that one bit," he said.

Just then a steamboat blew for the East Dubuque draw-bridge.

"What boat is that?" he said.

"Could be the *Mark Twain*," I said. "Or the *James W. Good*. They're both due through here about now."

And then the *Harriet* blew her landing whistle.

"And what boat is that?" he said.

"That's the *Harriet* coming in with sand from Nine Mile Island," I said.

"All right," he said. "I'll fix it with your mother."

Two days later we were in a box car on a Milwaukee freight enjoying the river view as we rumbled through North Buena Vista, Iowa. This was not part of the agreement, this was desperate he-man stuff. We rolled cigarettes with wheat straw papers and Bull Durham, and spit out of the box car onto the spider wort that grew beside the tracks. We were supposed to be in a Burlington day coach. Instead, we were with Grant at Vicksburg, we were with Peary at the pole, we were rounding Cape Horn in the *Flying Cloud* — we were bumming a freight train.

The first thing we found out in Winona was that there was no island across from town. At least no island that looked like a rafters' island. It was all unfamiliar. All of a sudden "making a raft" sounded not only foolish but impossible. We were standing on the riverbank there in Winona, Minnesota. That in itself was something, being in another state, a Northern state; this very state touched Canada. If we had been Huck and Tom, right about now a "little section of a lumber raft" would have appeared out of nowhere just for us. It would have been "twelve foot wide and about fifteen or sixteen foot long," with the top standing "above water six or seven inches, a solid level floor."*

But we weren't Tom and Huck, the last lumber raft had gone down the river in 1915, and the only thing that floated past was a rusty oil drum and the usual dead carp. There were some skiffs pulled up on the shore and we sat down on one to chew some Black Jack gum and think things over. Here we were about to cross the Rockies and we had no horses, no mules, no outfit.

"Not a bad flat boat," Al said, patting the gunwale of the boat we were sitting on. "What would you say, about sixteen feet?"

---

* Very unlikely. In the first place Sam Clemens should have remembered that "a little section of a lumber raft" was called a "crib." And also that a "crib" was a standard size of sixteen feet wide by thirty-two feet long. However, when you are producing rafts to order out of thin air in Hartford, Connecticut, I guess you can make them any size you want.

"Just about. She's not too limber, either," I said. "He's got her chained and padlocked to that hunk of limestone."

Al got up and looked at it.

"You know what I blieve," he said. "I blieve two people could pick that hunk of limestone right up and set her right in the boat."

"I blieve you're right, Huck," I said. "I blieve two people could do that."

"Mighty foolish for a person to be so particular about padlocks," Al said, "and at the same time leave a perfectly good pair of oars laying right there in plain view."

"No, it don't make much sense, Huck," I said.

So we went uptown and bought our outfit and put it in two gunny sacks and toted it down to the river and hid it in the weeds near that boat. The first thing we bought was a cold chisel and a hatchet; and then we bought a frying pan and a cooking pot and a flashlight and a lot of truck like that and a tarpaulin and a big spoon and knives and forks and canned goods and can opener and bread and cheese and Al saw a belt with studs on it so he bought that and I bought a compass and a scout knife in case we lost the can opener and I bought a straw hat and Al bought an old Harrington and Richardson .22 caliber revolver in a hock shop for seven dollars. You had to hand it to Al. The revolver added a lot of style.

We sat through two shows at the movies and before midnight we went back down there and put our gunny sacks in the boat, put the rock and chain in the boat and shoved off.

The drawbridge was right below on the Minnesota side. Naturally we didn't want that bridge-tender to see us so Al got busy with the oars and by the time we got down there to the bridge we were away out in the river and went through the third span. Then we put up the oars and drifted. It was so quiet you could hear a fish jump and fall back, over in the channel someplace.

When you are standing on the shore looking at it, the river seems to be moving along at a great clip but right now, having "lifted" or "borrowed" a skiff in the approved Bad Boy tradition we wanted to get out of there; but as Huckleberry once said, "the raft did seem to go mighty slow."

"It must have been onto one o'clock when we got below the island at last" and later than that before the lights of Winona began to dim away. We each took a turn at the oars, and smoked, and talked about it, and ate some cold beans and bread, and it was just like in The Book, sliding along down the Mississippi. We held over to the Wisconsin side and once in a while we would come down on a red nun buoy writhing to-and-fro in the dark with the current gurgling around it.

"We've gotta hide this boat and lay up for the day," Al said.

"Well don't I know that?" I said. "And we've got to cut willows."

So we did like it says in The Book:

"When the first streak of day begun to show, we tied up to a tow-head in a big bend on the Illinois [Wisconsin] side, and hacked off cotton-wood branches [willows] with the hatchet and covered up the raft [flat boat] with them so she looked like there had been a cave-in in the bank there."

It was a long time ago and I didn't know anything about the river then. I think we had a Light List, maybe not, but I know we didn't have any chart. We didn't have the charts on purpose; it would all be more mysterious without knowing what was around the next bend. And it was good that way since it was that kind of a trip. But ordinarily a chart is a good thing to have because it teaches you the names of things. As far as I can figure out after forty years, we must have tied up and hid out on that youthful day of long ago someplace below Trempealeau, Wisconsin, across from Island No. 86 — in there someplace.

And we were in luck, because there was an abandoned summer camp in there, with the shack up on stilts for the high water, and there was two old quilts in there, and a crummy mattress. We laid the mattress down in the stern end of the skiff and the quilts over it and that was our sleeping quarters the whole time. Then we took our tarp and rigged a tent over the bed. So we had a shelter at one end from the weather, our supplies in the bow, and one or the other of us amidships at the oars. It was beautiful. I wish I was back there right now.

This was in 1929, ten years nearly before the locks and dams and the present day pools of the Upper Mississippi. All, all was different. Recreational boating, which has now reached manic proportions, had barely been thought of. Pleasure boats were few, commercial fishermen and clammers scarce, and real live steamboats in short supply. Scattered over the 853 miles between the Northern Pacific Railroad bridge at Minneapolis and Peddies Landing at the mouth of the Ohio River there were probably not two dozen steamboats at work, including the ferry at Rock Island and the big railroad car ferry at Ste. Genevieve, Missouri. In addition there were: the struggling subsidized fleet of the Federal Barge Line; a number of small sternwheelers in the sand-and-gravel trade; the channel maintenance boats and dredges of the U.S. Government; and in the glamor dept., the *J.S.* and the *Capitol* of the Streckfus Lines, enormous, gaudy, tantalizing excursion boats with their steam calliopes and deep-throated whistles. High water and floods of spring were followed by extreme low water in summer making groundings frequent and navigation exasperating and a financial calamity.

So in 1929, before the dams made a permanent channel depth of nine feet, the river was in a relatively innocent and primitive condition, the valley in general old-fashioned and neglected. Can you imagine commercial fishermen with no power in their boats but oars? Children walked miles up the railroad tracks to school. Back yards were adorned with cistern pumps, kitchen sinks sported pitcher pumps which sometimes froze up because there was no heat in the kitchen at night. Wood-burning kitchen ranges and parlor base burners were not uncommon. Men wore long underwear. Houses had sheds behind them with sunflowers to the eaves. Front yards showed flowers planted in range boilers cut lengthwise. A good used Model-T Ford could be had for $10. Widows kept chickens. Sunday fun meant sitting in a rowboat fishing all day, watching a cork. Primitive characters abounded, and often frontier ways of doing things had not been improved upon. Ancient leathery persons thrived and Civil War veterans still tottered behind the town band on Memorial Day.

It was an idyllic situation and we relished it. It suited us. We thought it was just fine and loved every anachronism. We didn't know what had gone before, so we couldn't complain. We had never known the golden age of steamboating. How could we regret its passing? What steamboats there were satisfied us right down to the ground. *Now* we can look back, as George Byron Merrick did as long ago as 1909, and cry into our beer,* and tell sad tales of what used to be.

---

* All the old time breweries of the Upper Mississippi are gone now except at Dubuque and La Crosse. In former days towns as small as Cassville and Fountain City, Wisconsin, had their own breweries.

The majesty and glory of the Great River have departed [he said]. Its glamor remains, fresh and undying, in the memories of those who, with mind's eye, still can see it as it was half a century ago . . . its glamor is that indefinable witchery with which memory clothes the commonplace of long ago, transfiguring the labors, cares, responsibilities, and dangers of steamboat life as it really was, into a Midsummer Night's Dream of carefree, exhilarating experiences and glorified achievement.

Of the river itself it may be said, that like the wild tribes which peopled its banks sixty years ago, civilization has been its undoing.

It was ever so.

When Marquette and Joliet came out of the Wisconsin River and into the Mississippi on June 17, 1673, they were delighted.

"*Zut, alors, eh bien!*" they cried. "Thees wan reevair magnifique!"

"Yes, it's not bad," replied Pebblekicker the Indian guide, "but youse two ought to of saw it fifty years ago."

More than a century passed.

Lieutenant Zebulon Pike arrived at Julien Dubuque's lead mines at Catfish Creek in 1805.

"Mighty nice place you've got here, Monsoor Dubuque," he commented.

"Sank you, monsieur le Lieutenant," replied the handsome Frenchman handing Pike a souvenir hunk of lead, "but zee white man he haff, 'ow you say eet, fouled up zis environment."

"White man, what white man?" queried Pike.

"*Me voici*, I am zee white man," replied Julien.

And in Sam Clemens' time there was the river oracle and patriarch, Captain Isaiah Sellers, who fired off frequent informative paragraphs about navigational matters to the New Orleans *Picayune*, signing them "Mark Twain." In these articles the good captain never failed to make comparisons with the stage of the water in 1815 and peppered his comments with references to islands long since disappeared. He was also fond of phrases such as "When the State of Mississippi was where Arkansas now is" or "When Louisiana was up the river farther."

It's really great sport. When threading the buoys above the dam in the Dubuque pool of the present day, it's absolutely obligatory to tell some captive nephew or niece: "Well, you'd never guess it but we're right in the middle of what used to be Maquoketa Chute right this minute. See those stumps sticking out of the water over there? That used to be Riverside Gardens, a picnic spot and dancehall. Many the time I've danced out both my shoes over there. Oh this was a beautiful stretch of river back in those days."

Later on when they are alone Nephew No. 1 says to Nephew No. 2: "We went up through the pool on the *Coal Queen* and Uncle Dick told us again about Maquoketa Chute and how he used to dance out both his shoes at that dancehall."

"When you got up to Parsons Bar," says Nephew No. 2, "did he point out where Nick Balatz's place used to be in the old days?"

"Yep. He sure did."

But I Don't Care. We all do it and I am going to keep right on doing it. And these fresh kids have already got a start on it themselves, because when we were down the river in the *Nick* last summer we passed the foot of Island No. 230 and Nephew No. 1 says, "Uncle Dick, remember before the foot of the Island washed away and we used to camp over there and we had that big tree house? It sure was a pretty place, *back in those days*."*

That evening we turned loose and after dark we passed Dresbach and made the La Crescent railroad bridge and slid past the levee and the lights of La Crosse and figured we were all right, nobody would come looking for a flatboat in that wilderness below La Crosse. (Today there is a lock and dam at Dresbach and it would not be smart to take a borrowed flatboat through there; two kids in a flatboat would stick out like a catfish on Main Street.)

After that we relaxed and enjoyed life and ran days and tied up nights, except some nights when we ran for the romance of it all. It was hot and we were naked or half-naked most of the time and we swam a hundred times a day,† and foraged the islands and shot off Al's pistol, and the whole damn river valley was ours.

One thing we learned real fast and that was that in a flatboat on the Upper Mississippi you just don't do much drifting downstream — you have to *row*. The prevailing wind is from the south and it prevails most of the time even when there is not a breath stirring up in town. We hung an old canvas weighted with railroad iron over one end of the boat as a sea anchor to catch the current and it helped some, but not when the wind was brisk, not with that tent on the boat. Some days we gave up fighting it and just laid around all day on some island, or hung around in a little rivertown, sitting in the park by the river, maybe playing pool if they had a pool hall, or perhaps climbing up to the top of one of those

* Italics courtesy of the author.
† "What a summer! We must of drunk a thousand martinis!" — Copyright 1967 by J. D. Glab.

big high Upper Mississippi River bluffs to sit in the grass and flowers among the birch and cedar trees with the whole valley below us, the river winding away and away out of sight across the valley to the north.

There's a dreamy quality about the whole scene and it is not just nostalgia; it had a dreamy quality *then*. And we understood it and favored it and squeezed it for all it was worth. We were adventurers and we took notice. It wasn't a casual escapade or "something to do" until school started — it was the Big Parade, it was Lewis and Clark at the Three Forks.

Even today, on a lazy summer afternoon if you climb to the top of a cliff like Queens Bluff and look down at the river, all the headlines blur out for a while. There's the Mississippi rolling toward Dubuque and Hannibal and St. Louis, same as ever, and there's a towboat shoving coal to St. Paul — hell, maybe old Norm Hillman or Don Mullady or one of the boys is in the pilot house — and across the river a long Burlington freight is dragging along past the coulees under the Wisconsin bluffs, and for a while at least, if you squint your eyes a little so you can't see those goddam water skiers down there, nothing has changed.

Mark Twain went back to Hannibal after years as a wanderer. The visit wasn't a total success.

"That world which I knew in its blossoming youth is old and bowed and melancholy now; its soft cheeks are leathery and wrinkled, the fire is gone out in its eyes, and the spring from its step."

It was the changed town, and meeting people, that caused this outburst.

But at seven in the morning on a Sunday, he walked through the deserted streets:

and finally climbed Holiday's Hill to get a comprehensive view.

From this vantage ground the extensive view up and down the river, and wide over the wooded expanses of Illinois, is very beautiful — one of the most beautiful on the Mississippi, I think; which is a hazardous remark to make, for the eight hundred miles of river between St. Louis and St. Paul afford an unbroken succession of lovely pictures. . . . It was satisfyingly beautiful to me, and it had this advantage over all the other friends whom I was about to greet again: it had suffered no change; it was as young and fresh and comely and gracious as ever it had been. *

According to the prescription we should all the way down have been incessantly catching fish and frying them. We never baited a hook. And we ought to have been making corn dodgers, johnny cake, and sourdough biscuits; baking potatoes in the coals and roasting corn; snaring rabbits, spearing turtles, shooting squirrels; making mulligan stew and bean hole beans.

But we didn't.

We tried for awhile to emulate Huck and Tom by stealing things to eat but we didn't know what to do with them. What can two kids in a rowboat do with five summer squashes? Feeling an obligation to the Real American Boy tradition and to Huckleberryism we determined to steal a watermelon. Where *are* the watermelon patches of the Upper Mississippi? We couldn't find one.

We camped often, made complicated Dan Beard fires and fireplaces, and lived on canned soup, canned hash, canned beans, something awful called canned Irish stew, something even worse called canned spaghetti, and lots of canned chili, canned sardines, canned herring in tomato sauce, and canned

* It's not 800 miles from St. Louis to St. Paul, it is 660 miles.

salmon which we ate right out of the can. We put away a whole lot of patent squush bread with peanut butter and strawberry jam. Once in a while we cut willow sticks and blackened a few wieners. Pushing authenticity we boiled coffee in a lard pail but gave that up presently by admitting that we neither of us liked coffee. A case of soda pop lasted us about 24 hours. A guy in Alma sold us some home brew. We chalked up a lot of personal credit from this desperate move but in the long run it made, of me at least, a "Less than One Beer Man" for life.

Unlike Huckleberry we had money in our pockets and we weren't hiding out so we went ashore in those little towns "drowsing in the sun" and sat right down in the Romance Cafe or the Riverside Lunch or the EAT and had some ham and eggs doused in ketchup or a cowboy steak and three bottles of ice cold assorted sody pop.

The islands of the Mississippi belong to the government. That doesn't mean you and me, it means the government. In 1973 if you tie your houseboat up to the shore of an island for a few months, the govment sends you a god damn *bill*. "Call this a govment," as Pap Finn used to say when the liquor started to work. "Oh yes, this is a wonderful govment, wonderful."

What was it like there on those islands of the upper river? It was like this:

We cut up past the black buoys and crossed over to Minnesota Island, ran her in and tied off to a cottonwood root. I took the ax and we climbed up the bank and walked under the trees; it was soft and warm and smothery in there, with the smell of mud and burdock leaves, nettles, wild grapevines, bugs and sink holes, a few flowers, rotten logs, pregnant toadstools, and the mosquitoes, who greeted us with a long cheer for the team.

Although the Ford Hopkins drugstore was only a few miles away, and from under the still trees we could see the semi-trailer trucks burning up the slab across the river on their way to Winona, here on our musky island it was tangled and wild, and the cottonwoods and elms, existing only for the pleasure of the bluejays who frolicked in their upper branches, were poised like lithographic, old-fashioned trees overburdened with foliage. Under the loose bark of dead trees the bugs pursued their dismal calling, while in the rich alluvium underfoot blind worms slid sightlessly on moist and endless errands . . .

We walked across the jungly island and on the far side, by the sweet stagnant slough, a big gar pike lay stranded in the shore mud, with his long snout desiccating in the summer sun and his soul in hell. Beyond, with the salamanders creeping stupidly among their roots, the lotus bloomed and filled the air with whiffs of the ancient Nile. God, Mohammed, or Zoroaster perhaps could give a complete inventory of what lay beneath the surface of that wide and slimy pool, and if any of them knew I hoped they would keep it to themselves. A water snake went horribly squirming through the green plankton . . .

Leaving the fringe-finned ganoids and the gar pike and snake, we went away from the hot prehistoric expanse of trapped water and made our way back through the whirring insects to the shaded alleys beneath the trees. Clubbing a path through the nettles and eager undergrowth, we came at last to a half-open, park-like place beside the river, where the trunks of the trees rose high in search of the sun, and the shade restricted the ground cover to sickly grasses and pale flowers.

There was an old fisherman's camp in there, with a shanty up on stilts to keep it above the high water. We combed it over but there was nothing there except a busted Dietz lantern, a pair of old rubber boots with holes, and some rusted-out tin plates. A 1926 coal and ice dealer's calendar was hanging behind the door — no wonder there was not much left. Joe was set on getting something though, so he took along an old file he found in the woods.

We picked out a good straight elm about twenty-five feet high. Joe grabbed the ax and commenced to work out some of his high spirits on it, and the chips began to fly. A blue racer slid for cover into the brush. The tree gave up and came down with a swish.

We stripped the tree and dragged the pole over to the river; it didn't set so good on the boat, so we decided to tow it out when the boat came along. She was just heading through the drawbridge, about a mile down river, her eight loads setting down low in the water and creeping along against the current. We sat down on the bank and had a smoke and cooled off and we talked about whether snakes were good to have around a farm or not. I told Joe there was no such thing as a hoop snake, but he said his uncle saw one down in Illinois on his farm . . .

Across the fluttering water at River Junction a big Milwaukee freight was heading up the line with about seventy-five cars from all over — the Nickel Plate, the Erie, the Pere Marquette, the Seaboard Airline, Canadian National, D & R G W, Vermont Central, B & O, Boston and Maine . . .

Over it all was the sweet hot smell of the river and the islands, of the cottonwoods and wild grapes, and the rich dark mud from the north, brought down to the river by so many little creeks from the prairies.

That rather fancy piece of prose is from my famous "Banned in Dubuque" novel of 1950, *A Stretch on the River*. This part was presumably not banned although it does contain the words "pregnant" and "hell." If you think it is odd for me to quote from my own works, Mark Twain gave me the clue. In *Life on the Mississippi*, right off the bat in Chapter Three he quotes 19 pages from a book which hadn't even been published yet, *Huckleberry Finn*.

At Lansing where Main Street runs right down into the river I walked up the street at 5 AM one morning. The sun was up but there was nobody stirring except at the bakery. I was barefooted and all I had on was overhalls and a shirt with the sleeves torn off. I went in the bakery and bought some hot rolls from the baker and went out and sat on the curbstone in front of the Model Clothing Store and ate those buns. That's the time I really felt like Huckleberry, a wanderer, a gypsy of the valley. In the soft sweet warm air of the pink Wisconsin dawn.

We stayed overnight in the old Dennison House at Cassville. We got a room on the third floor with a million bats in the walls for $1.50. After supper we sat on the porch in front, looking at the river. There were some engineers there, civil engineers, in tan shirts and pants, with Southwestern accents. They were surveying the river for the government, for the locks and dams which were then only in the planning stage. The sun went down over the Turkey River bottoms and in the dusk their soft voices and laughter floated back and forth. They had been on jobs everywhere: Peru, Russia, Afghanistan. . . . The *General Ashburn* passed upriver; the Mormon flies swirled around the street light at the corner; the river rolled on, it never lets up.

When we got to Dubuque we went right on past. We knew that, if we showed ourselves, our folks would say we had had enough. But we hadn't. We never did, and we probably never will.

We tied up to a float at Clinton, Iowa, and went uptown. While we were gone the Federal Barges Lines' big sternwheeler *Patrick Hurley* went by and her wheel wash flipped the boat. Everything was gone. We decided to quit. It was a buyer's market on overturned boats and we sold her for three dollars.

We had visualized coming into Hannibal in glory, by flatboat all the way from Minnesota. That was out but we would continue and complete the holy pilgrimage anyway.

We bummed a freight to Galesburg, Illinois. From Galesburg we rode the bumpers to Quincy. From Quincy we grabbed a reefer to Hannibal, where we walked right into the Hotel Mark Twain in our hobo regalia and checked in.

Where it said "Home Address" we both wrote "Winona, Minnesota."

ELEVEN

All These Royal Pleasures

I was born the 30th of November, 1835, in the almost invisible village of Florida, Monroe County, Missouri.

An almost invisible two-room frame house was the scene of this important literary event. There is no way to glamorize this pathetic shack. It was simply miserable. And in addition to its pitiful appearance and accommodations it lacked a further ingredient. Most of the houses in Florida were of logs but Mark Twain had the bad luck to be born in one of the only frame houses in town, another example of his father John Clemens' poor planning against the day when the infant would take his honorary degree from Oxford. Sweet as it was, how much sweeter it would have been if the world-famous recipient's birthplace had been made of logs. Herbert Hoover was robbed of the same cachet when his Quaker parents arranged for him to be born, in 1874, in another such microscopic frame kennel, in West Branch, Iowa, a structure of boards even closer to invisibility than the Clemens coop. Both men achieved highest honors despite the lack of log-cabin nativity, and in his old age Hoover's face took on the aspect of a wistful baked apple.

Moving out of dreary, mud-bespattered, dejected poke-town four years later to the bright lights of Hannibal-on-the-Mississippi, John Clemens dribbled along and in the 1840's built a house at 206 Hill Street. This house stands today as a Mark Twain museum and is another lilliputian barracks by nearly any standards, but a chateau in Xanadu compared to the shriveled-up hutch 85 miles way, back in Florida on the Salt River. (Likewise a nearly imperceptible stream although John Clemens had dreams, like all the Clemenses, and was a big mover in the nebulous Salt River Navigation Company.)

Originally this was only a one-story structure but after Clemens senior died, in 1847 at the end of a mortifying life, slap-happy Orion Clemens, a loser like his father, added a story on top and operated his pathetic print shop and woeful weekly newspaper up there. It is here that the character of America's most famous literary good-bad boy, Tom Sawyer, was born and out of this window right here, we are told, an eleven- or twelve-year-old kid not only escaped undetected from the house practically every night by opening a window and sliding down a downspout, but regained his room several hours later without waking up a living soul, by *climbing up* the downspout.

This is palpably impossible and far harder to take than James Fenimore Cooper's Indians, who, to Twain's indignation, couldn't jump into a canal boat six feet beneath them without missing and falling into the water. It is plainly impossible, yet I have never heard anyone question such unlikely juvenile gymnastics, even Leslie Fiedler, although he is very interested in just exactly what Huck and Nigger Jim's emotional involvement was on that raft. (I know but I'm not saying. Send 25 cents in stamps for this information which will be mailed in plain wrappers.)

Sam Clemens presently shook loose from the Missouri

dust and deep black mud and went wandering; and met Governors and Bankers and actual Kings, Kings whom he as a stars-and-stripes democrat affected to belittle but who actually gave him his supreme and final *frisson;* and became famous and made eighteen crossings of the Atlantic. Leaving behind him forever these humblest of hogans in Missouri, the state with the funny connotations, the "show me" state, lair of the comical "Missouri mule." Never again would he live in such humiliating digs, not on the seedy steamer *Paul Jones*, not on De Voto's "mineral frontier" in Nevada, not in San Francisco. Living in a shanty in the silver mines is Romance, living in a shanty in your hometown is gall, wormwood, and pignuts.

He left town with a sixpence and a spare homespun shirt tied up in a bandanna. Twenty-one years later he built and moved into an ostentatious twenty-room house of bizarre aspects in Hartford, Connecticut, which required a staff of six to keep it in motion. He had got rich. And as my old classmate Wayne Andrews, architecture historian, says of the period, "the masters of new fortunes looked for new ways to impress their neighbors with their importance." In Mark Twain's case the house advertised to the levee loungers back home his new, elevated refinement. "New England! Connecticut! Hartford! Why, it's almost Boston!" It hung out a sign that he wanted from now on to have some respect around here, and even a little worship. If the house wouldn't do the trick he was prepared to nail his bank statement to a tree on Farmington Avenue. This was wiping out the past with a great, feckless insistence that would go on until April 1910 when he would die in another large house, in the stupid, alien, imitation-rural hills of southern Connecticut.

When Dan De Quille was staying with Mark Twain in Hartford in 1875, writing *The Big Bonanza*, he wrote to his sister back home in Iowa: "I think I have conquered my awe of these New Englanders and the grand old city of Hartford. . . . They are very religious here — they worship God and greenbacks. Greenbacks six days in the week, and God all the spare time they can find on the remaining day."

Meanwhile:

The plans for the new house were drawn forthwith by that gentle architect Edward Potter [says Albert Bigelow Paine] whose art today* may be considered open to criticism, but not because of any lack of originality. Hartford houses of that period were mainly of the goods-box form of architecture, perfectly square, typifying the commercial pursuits of many of their owners. Potter agreed to get away from this idea, and a radical and even frenzied departure was the result. Certainly his plans presented beautiful pictures, and all who saw them were filled with wonder and delight.

Wayne Andrews also has a unique definition of architectural taste in *Architecture, Ambition, and Americans*, which fits this occasion neatly: "Taste is the record of the ambition which leads the architect to spend more time and energy than is reasonable, and the client . . . to invest more money than common sense would direct."

Mark Twain, a mere journalist and popular lecturer at this time, paid $31,000 for the five acres of land, $21,000 for the furniture, and $70,000 for the house. Add to this a staff of no less than six servants, a carriage and pair, and the usual extras — then triple the total to make the figures meaningful for the 1970's, and smite your forehead. And the wonderful thing is, he pulled it off! The Clemens family lived here from 1874 to 1891, seventeen years, before his crazy speculations and goofy business ventures — always accompanied by dreams of increased glory — burst the lovely bubble.

* "Today" was 1912.

In the meantime he had seventeen productive literary years, and seventeen years of domestic rapture. It was during the Farmington Avenue period that he did nearly all his significant work: *Tom Sawyer*, *A Tramp Abroad*, *A Connecticut Yankee in King Arthur's Court*, *The Prince and the Pauper*, *Life on the Mississippi*, and *Huckleberry Finn* were all written during these years in "the loveliest home that ever was . . . bewitchingly bright and splendid and homelike." Three of these works are among the most famous books ever written since people began scratching on stones and mud tablets. Based on the quality of his literary production after leaving Farmington Avenue, it seems obvious that no matter what, he "should of stood at home."

The Hartford *Daily Times* of March 23, 1874, gives a progress report of the strange doings out on the Avenue:

Most of the residents of Hartford know that Mr. Samuel H. [*sic*] Clemens, otherwise known as "Mark Twain," is building a residence on Farmington Avenue, a short distance east of the stone bridge on that thoroughfare. Many of the readers of the *Times*, doubtless, have had at least an external view of the structure, which already has acquired something beyond a local fame; and such persons, we think, will agree with us in the opinion that it is one of the oddest looking buildings in the State ever designed for a dwelling, if not in the whole country. From an inspection of the building, now fast approaching completion, we are able to give the following description of it:

It is located on a lot of ground some 612 feet by about 400, just west of Forest Street, being on the south side of Farmington Avenue. It is of brick, and three stories in height, fronting easterly. The extreme length of the building is 105 feet 4 inches; its extreme width 62 feet 4 inches. On the west side there is an octagonal tower 48 or 50 feet in height; while at the extreme ends, north and south, of the house, there are towers of less height. The designs for the building were furnished by Edward T. Potter and Alfred H. Thorp, Architects, of New York. On the first floor there is to be a parlor, drawing room or library, dining room and bedrooms. The drawing room, on the rear of the south end of the building, is to open into a semi circular conservatory. On the second floor there will be a study, nursery, sewing room and boudoir, housekeeper's room, servants' bedroom, and numerous bathrooms. On the third floor there will be a billiard room, artists' friends' room, toilet and two servants' rooms. The dining room, at the rear, on the north end of the house, has one feature we do not recollect to have seen in any other building, and that is a window directly above a fireplace. From it a pleasant view on the avenue is to be obtained. There are no less than five balconies about this building, beside that of the west tower. A verandah will run around the south end and the east front of the ground floor of the building, with an extensive covered projection or porte cochere (driveway for carriages) on the east. The rooms will all be finished in black walnut and oak, except the nursery and bathrooms, in which butternut will be used. The main hallway of the building, open from the first floor to the third, is 15 by 25 feet; and this gives promise of being a very fine portion of the structure . . .

The novelty displayed in the architecture of the building, the oddity of its internal arrangement, and the fame of its owner, will all conspire to make it a house of note for a long time to come.

William Dean Howells, down from Boston, looked on and approved: "Clemens was then building the stately mansion in which he satisfied his love of magnificence as if it had been another sealskin coat, and he was at the crest of the prosperity which enabled him to humor every whim or extravagance."

People came, saw and were conquered. It was a great

coup. Like his lectures it had been carefully constructed to give off entertainment and joy. I have never heard of George P. Lathrop, but he was Nathaniel Hawthorne's son-in-law. He went crackers over the entrance hall:

And a charming haunt it is, with its wide hall, finished in dark wood under a paneled ceiling, and full of easy chairs, rugs, cushions, and carved furniture that instantly invite the guest to lounge in front of the big fireplace. But it is a house made for hospitality, and one cannot stop at that point. Over the fireplace, through a large plate-glass suggesting Alice's Adventures, a glimpse is had of the drawing room, luminous with white and silver and pale blue; and on another side, between a broad flight of stairs and a chiseled Ginevra chest drawn against the wall, the always open library door attracts one's steps.

They came from far and near. Even the Big Town succumbed. A reporter from the New York *World* got mushy over the billiard room:

This room is a treat. A big billiard table with black and gold legs stands in the middle of it. Its windows look to the westward over a festive and noisy brook in a setting of rich, green turf, past clumps of elm and birch and oak and maple. A long line of high blue hills marks the western horizon. On the other side of them is the Farmington Valley. Close at hand the robins' nests on a tall beech seem likely to fall in at the window. It is a delightful spot altogether, just the place for hard work.

Without children a house is nothing. That's why so many houses and palaces and cleverly decorated apartments in full color in *Vogue* and *Town and Country* are nothing. *My own houses are nothing* because the pitter patter of little tootsies, and jam sandwiches on the sofa are things of the past. The house on Farmington Avenue had Susy, Jean, and Clara Clemens and their playmates. Clara, the only daughter to survive Mark Twain, recalled the "school room" on the second floor:

Our school room provided memories never to be repeated. Snowstorms raging about the many windows, against which a fire on the hearth cozily defended us. And our Shakespeare club! Oh, the wonderful plays we produced with a larger cast of actors than auditors! Memory test of books we had read and hated. Recitations of poetry we adored. Concerts performed on our baby upright. But, best of all, popcorn and roasted chestnuts! All these royal pleasures in a room modestly called the school room.

It is indeed a make-believe house, a brownie house, a house for little girls peeping over balustrades and calling down from secret balconies, a house drenched in cottage charm and that "Picturesque Eclecticism" so dear to the eager hearts of the High Victorians.

But was it all as "odd" as that reporter for the Hartford paper said it was? "Perhaps the oddest building ever built in the U.S.A.," he said. A novelty, a curiosity.

But was it all that different? By the 1870's America had produced dozens of circus varieties of flamboyant architecture.

It is not as lavish as "Lyndhurst," that magnificent gothic seat in Tarrytown. (1838)

It is nowheres near as pretentious as the J. B. Chollar house in Watervliet, New York. (1848)

How about the Wedding Cake house in Kennebunk, Maine, a house of lace? (1845)

H. H. Richardson and others were designing many grandiose dwellings in this period with opulent interiors of stunning complexity.

And there's spook haven, "Longwood," in Natchez, Mississippi, that moorish monument to vanity and ruination. (1860)

And "Olana," Frederick Church's castle on the Hudson which also boasts fancy brickwork effects like The House That Mark Built. (1871). Truly a sumptuous pleasure dome.

In the matter of stepped gables, italianate windows and elegant chimneys there was Washington Irving's snuggery, "Sunnyside," also at Tarrytown. Everyone was familiar with it. It is by no means ordinary. (1832)

And as a matter of fact the English Perpendicular Gothic Villa, with its barge boards, brackets, oriels, turrets, bay windows, massy chimneys, lacy eaves and tracery in windows had pleasingly invaded the land in the 1840's and 1850's and what is the house at 351 Farmington Avenue but this style freely translated into patterned brick? Even the steep pitched gables are there. Or, with its bands of color, outlandish brickwork and dollhouse facade is it a showy variant of the Second Empire style of Louis Napoleon? Think for a moment of the old Winnipeg, Manitoba, City Hall for example. (R.I.P. 1962). If you can't think of it, pretend you're in Graduate School, rub your pipe on your nose and nod your head thoughtfully. At any rate, or "in any event" as Anastasia Bissell says, it's all medieval and lush and cozy and located in HARTFORD, CONNECTICUT, where the QUALITY come from it is not on the far banks of the Mississippi or anything like. And there are six servants and a conservatory with a fountain, and a huge carved mantel from a castle in Scotland, what do you think of that?

Even so the lord of the manse was not entirely satisfied.

No one with a royal residence ever is. (Bissell Manor in Dubuque has been worked over and altered and fiddled with and redecorated a dozen times in the past eighty years.) So in a very few years King Clemens the First summoned the minions of the Duke of Tiffany to his regal presence, as told in *Louis C. Tiffany, Rebel in Glass* by Robert Koch.

In the summer of 1881 Louis Tiffany and Candace Wheeler redecorated Samuel Clemens' (Mark Twain's) home in Hartford, Connecticut, by adding stenciled decorations designed after Indian motifs to walls and ceilings. As Mark Twain wrote early that spring, the Farmington Avenue house, not ten years old, would be given a more up-to-date look: "In June we shall tear out the reception room to make our front hall bigger . . . and at the same time the decorator will decorate the walls and ceilings of our whole lower floor." The original stencil work may still be seen on the panels of walls and doors; some of the tiles are duplicates of those used in the Armory and other Tiffany interiors.

For the dining room fireplace, above which a window was placed at the author's suggestion where he "could watch the flames leap to reach the falling snowflakes," Tiffany supplied tiles in three different colors — turquoise, amber, and brown — in a combination of transparent and opaque glass. When the work had been completed Tiffany's famous client sent him a check and a note "I have been down on the Mississippi River or I would have answered sooner. I am happy to say that the work is not merely and coldly satisfactory, but intensely so."

The entrance hall has the required gloom and heaviness and imitation associated with new accumulations of unexpected cash and a desire to be strictly high class. My grandfather's house on West Third Street gave off the same odors of Illinois Central Railroad bonds with its heavily beamed and paneled ceiling, its Rutherford B. Hayes rococo fireplace, and the "Persian Corner." I don't know why Mark Twain had no "Persian Corner" in his house, but he did have an unusually somber black Venetian bed, heavily carved, with cherubs who peeked at Sam Clemens as he sat in bed puffing stogies in his nightshirt. As a "Parvenu Period" piece it is in a perfect setting. It was his Majestical Bed.

Many people who admire Mark Twain and like this house in Hartford keep telling me that the interior staircase and stair well are "like on a steamboat." I have protested, and even got the curator, a few years back, to cease and desist from this allegation and to go stand in a corner. The staircase of the House on Farmington Avenue is in an open three-story stair well just exactly like the one on West Third Street in Dubuque and the stairs go around and around until they get to the top, where they stop and everybody goes into the billiard room and says, "Pick a cue." On a steamboat the staircase swoops right up from the main deck forward straight up to the boiler deck. No curves, bends, corkscrew effects, or electroliers. It just rises up in a grand manner and hearts are gay. But it doesn't look like, or influence in any way, Mark Twain's staircase.

As for the "boiler deck," since the boilers are, and always have been, on the deck below the "boiler deck," steamboat historians have a good time thinking up explanations. The most popular is that if the boilers blow up and you are on the "boiler deck" above them you will get the full treatment and go two miles in the air and land in somebody's soy-bean futures.

Another enthusiast says the house has a porch "like the deck of a steamboat." What it has is a nice piazza which has less to do with steamboat architecture than my foot. Somebody has got to scotch these feeble legends, invented by desperate journalists who have never been any closer to a Mississippi steamboat than the precinct rumshop.

Up in Elmira, New York, where he spent summers with his wife Livy's sister, Mrs. Theodore Crane, Mark had his famous study, separated from the house and sitting as he said, "perched in complete isolation on top of an elevation that commands leagues of valley and city and retreating ranges of distant blue hills." Although this building is *octagonal* and has a *peaked roof*, it has been mandatory for several generations of boob explainers to describe it as "shaped like a pilot house" or "built like a pilot house." It is about as much like a pilot house as my other foot.

Happily I have, after exhaustive research in the Bibliotheque Nationale and the British Museum found one scholar who says what it really is. In his sensible pictorial history of Victorian America, *The Gingerbread Age*, John Maas lays it on the line: "Mark Twain's famous octagonal study is supposedly patterned after a riverboat pilot's cabin but looks like most Victorian summerhouses and bandstands."

In 1891, the same year my grandfather's mansion with its billiard room, speaking tubes, and butler's pantry was finished in Dubuque, Mark Twain left the house in Hartford never to return. "The maintenance was far too costly for his present and prospective income," says his biographer Paine. "The house with its associations of seventeen incomparable years must be closed. A great period had ended."

He went abroad for years, this most American of all Americans who ever lived, and occupied damp palaces in Italy, furnished flats in Paris, hotels everywhere (and he hated hotels). Terribly strange behavior. Couldn't he have pulled in his belt, fired half the servants, knocked off the incessant entertaining, the twenty-pound rib roasts, the champagne suppers, the midnight wassail bowls? Was wandering around Europe for years actually all that much cheaper a way to live? *Mon dieu!* Think of the tips alone!!

The house stood empty for years.

In 1903 it was sold to Richard H. Bissell, president of the Hartford Fire Insurance Co., august member of that great New England consanguinity (Windsor, Connecticut, 1628) to which the present writer belongs.

Cousin Richard lived there until 1917, when it was rented to a private school for boys.

Bissell sold it in 1922 and it was used as a (*shudder*) storage warehouse, then as a (*gasp, groan*) rooming house.

Finally — about time there, folks — a civic group called the Mark Twain Memorial Committee bought it in 1929 from the City Coal Company, who were using it as a depot for defective lumps of Number Nine coal.

It is now a museum, admission $1. Nothing has been spared to make it one of the finest restoration jobs anyone could possibly ask for. It's gorgeous, and the staff is proud, chatty, and dedicated.

"The spirits of the dead hallow a house for me," Mark Twain said in a posthumous piece in *Harper's Magazine* in January, 1911. "Susy died in the house we built in Hartford. Mrs. Clemens would never enter it again. But it made the house dearer to me. I visited it once since; when it was tenantless and forlorn, but to me it was a holy place and beautiful."

LUDWIG LEWISOHN
ON SAMUEL AND OLIVIA CLEMENS

"He married her in early 1870 and established that lavish and splendid and, on a high plane, inimitably Micawberish mode of life that continued to the end."

TWELVE

A 15,000 Watt Coffeepot

Fred Way tried to warn me — *Captain* Fred Way, that is. When I told him I was going to have a towboat built at the Dubuque Boat and Boiler Company he said "Oh oh" and tried to steer me off it but I wouldn't listen I had to have that towboat. Besides, hadn't Hank Miller, president of the Dubuque Boat and Boiler Works shown me those pages all covered with figures *proving* that a harbor boat at Dubuque would reap enormous profits?

This was a masterful document. Hank had started his commercial career in a Chicago or possibly a South Bend bank — he had quite by chance become a shipbuilding tycoon: in fact he had married a shipyard. Well, he married Doris and Doris had a shipyard, with two steam cranes. He was soon talking in a loud earnest voice about diesel injectors, McCabe Flanger machines, and propeller pitches — with all the pompous authority of a plumber's apprentice — and writing down lists of figures and adding them up and "recapping" and "projecting" them the way he had learned how to do in the bank and it was very impressive. After all I am just a very creative-type-person and a poet-pilot, not a mathematician. So I studied his figures and looked serious and made some marks on a piece of paper of my own, something I learned when I was in the manufacturing business at "Glovers." Henry was rasping through his scape pipes. He knew I had a bankroll and he wanted the job for the yard.

He grew pale with anxiety. I feared the advent of Cheyne-Stokes breathing, coma, apnea . . .

"Well, Henry," I said, "if a switch boat at Dubuque will be such a gold mine, then why don't you build one and operate it yourself. Hell I don't even live here."

"Captain, I'm a boat builder," he said. "You're a pilot, you're a steamboat man."

As a lifelong purveyor of gull toddy this was his finest hour.

Captain Fred Way, Jr., of Sewickley, Pennsylvania, over on the Ohio River had got the idea years before that he wanted to own a packet boat on the Ohio River. He bought the pretty little steamer *Betsy Ann* and entered into the adventure with all the zest and enthusiasm of a kid with a new Lionel train, only for real. The times were wrong, however, the age of passenger and short-haul-freight business by steamboat on the Ohio was fast slipping away. It kept slipping faster and soon it was about gone altogether and he went bust. With great good humor and in his inimitable style he told of this in an inland waterway classic called *The Log of the Betsy Ann.*

Of course I had read it, everybody had read it and chuckled over it, and was a bit sad, too, that he didn't make it, couldn't make it and after such a valiant try; that those beautiful packet days were gone forever. I often think of the end of that book. He has finally, heartbreakingly sold the precious *Betsy Ann:*

I discovered myself sitting in the park at Memphis. Sitting there looking out over the bar at the mouth of Wolf River and watching smoke curl from the fancy-topped stacks of my boat. The whistle blew. . . . It was then evident that she was going away and that I had nothing to do with the matter. Nobody had come and asked the familiar "Are you ready, Cap? . . ."

There was a thunderstorm brewing. Soon it commenced to rain, a gentle, warm spring rain. I found myself wondering if any of the rooms were leaking on the *Betsy;* whether the texas windows were shut.

THE END

But the *Betsy Ann* didn't have anything to do with switch-boats — that's what I was going to build — or with coal barges, molasses barges, oil barges, grain barges, tallow barges — or with barge lines. Dubuque was unloading a few hundred barges a year at this time and the idea was this: when a big towboat with from eight to twenty barges arrived in town with a single barge to deliver they had to tie off the whole string of barges below town and use a huge 5,000 horsepower towboat and two hours to deliver one measly barge or maybe two. My "switchboat" would go out and snatch the barge away from them instead, and they would go on up the river, or down the river. And I would send them a bill for $35 for delivering the barge. And I would own a genuine towboat and it would pay off and everybody would have a lot of fun. Well we had a lot of fun, a great deal of it at my expense, and it didn't pay off. I didn't go bust but I ended up fairly well bent, just like the rudders.

The Bissell Towing and Transport Co., incorporated in the State of New York, came into being. All you have to do to become a Corporation is to get some lawyers in a room and they will incorporate your dishwasher if you ask them to in a nice way and pay them enough money. Of course they will tell you it's going to be very difficult but they say they will pull it off because they have big licenses on the wall framed under glass and you haven't. Your pilot's license isn't worth a damn for forming a Corporation. Before the keel for the new towboat is laid you receive a bill for legal services which puts you into bankruptcy immediately.

But the bankers, some of whom wear actual vests and watch chains, are very friendly and keep stuffing your pockets with bills of large denominations and saying, "Sign here. Miss Munchkin will you please witness this signature?"

You will not be surprised to hear that these philanthropic bankers were not hometown bankers. There's a well-known law of economics which states that it is unethical for hometown banks to give you as good a deal as you can get in Chicago or Cincinnati. Mammoth Flange Inc. of Detroit gets its loans from the Manufacturers Hanover in New York and when the Hanover borrows some money with which to buy Ecuador they get it from the First Third Union of Dubuque and when the First Third of Dubuque decides to splatter fifteen drive-in branch banks over the country they borrow the dough from the Farmers Bank of Mineral Point, Wisconsin. I tried one Dubuque bank but they grew pale and fidgety and asked me how my mother was, so I got the money for the boat from the popular Pulp Cutters Trust Co. of Caribou, Maine.

Mark Twain paid out about $300,000 in all to a get-rich scheme called the Paige Typesetter. When it was all over he had nothing except a model of this useless gadget worth about 8 dollars for scrap iron. This is still in the basement of the house in Hartford. When I was through I had the towboat which I sold for $35,000. Since I had paid

$60,000 for the boat ten years before I did pretty good. And based on the price of a new car that has to be "recalled" every few months it wasn't all that costly either. And think of the warm thrills of satisfaction I presented to the cheering section who stood in the wings waiting for me to fall on my face. Did I have $25,000 worth of fun? Yes.

The blueprints arrived. The contract was for $45,000 but by the time I got through with the blueprints I had added ten feet overall to the length of the boat, plus a galley and bunk room and some other doodads and the cost ended up around $60,000. But we had it the way I wanted it, just like Mr. Blandings and his house.

"This is my Dream Boat and I'm not going to pare cheese," was the way I put it.

"I hope you know what you're doing," was my wife's rejoinder to this stout-hearted proclamation.

One thing Mark Twain and I share besides our pilot's licenses: we were both born and raised (270 miles away from each other) on the Upper Mississippi but we both ended up living in Connecticut. He picked it, I fell into it by chance. I still live there but I have a secret plan, which I can't divulge until after I'm elected, to escape from the New Haven Railroad any day now, possibly to a suite at the George Sank in Paris, France, and if I do I will not return in one year crestfallen and disillusioned like my friend Dr. Perelman.

So here I was having a towboat built, and going into business 1,200 miles away from Bat's Tavern and Shanty Inn on the Norwalk River, Connecticut. Not my home, exactly, but definitely in the neighborhood. Let me tell you right now that absentee ownership is all for the seagulls. Take shrimp cocktails for instance. Now if I had been there . . .

The launching was a magnificent success and due to my

tremendous fame as a writer, bomber pilot, choreographer, and Olympic pole vaulter it made the local paper with pictures of the big splash and also the Des Moines *Register*.

A month later the boat was finished and ready for a trial run. It was painted a lovely red like the Moran tugboats in New York harbor with black trim and BISSELL TOWING AND TRANSPORT CO. in letters a foot high running along both sides of the boat. The name on the pilot house could also be read a mile away. The name was *Coal Queen* in fond recollection of the first piece of writing I ever sold, which burst like an aerial bomb over the astonished heads of the readers of the *Atlantic Monthly*, Edward Weeks, editor. Seventy-five years previously, Mark Twain's first sections of *Life on the Mississippi* had appeared in this same very elevated and Bostonian literary dreadnought, William Dean Howells, pilot and chief engineer. "The *Coal Queen*" was about towboat life on the Monongahela River in West Virginia, where I had put in time. It did for me in my modest way what "The Celebrated Jumping Frog of Calaveras County" did for Sam Clemens. After that there was no turning back and no further thoughts of sending that coupon to the Coyne Electrical School at 500 South Paulina St. in Chicago to find out the Quick, Easier Way to MAKE BIG MONEY IN ELECTRICITY!! I was a Writer.

So I named the boat *Coal Queen*. Maybe I should have christened it the *Edward Weeks*, making it the first towboat on western waters ever named for an editor of the *Atlantic Monthly*. But we already had the sternwheeler *John W. Weeks* of the Federal Barge Line, named for an ex-Secretary of War who received 105 votes for the presidential nomination in the Republican National Convention of 1916. No use in crowding the field.

The shakedown cruise turned out to be shakier than expected with overtones of near tragedy. I arrived in East Dubuque on the Burlington Zephyr or rather *in* the Burlington Zephyr, *in* the bar car with some legionnaires from St. Paul who had adopted me on the way through Oregon, Illinois, and elected me Mayor of St. Paul.

When I got to the shipyard and went aboard I found the pilot house so full of shipyard personnel and relatives that the walls were buckling. The engine service man from the Caterpillar factory was tuning up the engines and fussing around with his stethoscope and tongue depressors and he kept at this until it got dark and I said this is no time to shake down my boat I am going up the hill and we will give her a spin tomorrow.

"Oh no," they said, "there is a tow coming up and we have got to take a load of coal from them and deliver it to Interstate and see how she handles a load and take an empty out of Interstate and see how she handles an empty and like that there."

The pilot house was right over the engine room and there was a staircase down but the architect had forgotten to include a hatch to close it so that what with two giant diesel engines and the high-speed diesel generator the whole scene was like making conversation inside the Dubuque Lumber and Coal Company's rock crusher.

"And besides," they screamed, "you have got to let them know you are ready to give them service. And start making money."

"Listen," I shrieked, "they haven't had a switchboat here in a hundred and fifty years why can't they wait twelve more hours until tomorrow?"

"Oh *they* can wait but you can't you have to move something and start making some money."

We took her out. Hank Miller, genial shipyard owner, had

aboard his personal private pilot, Captain T. Trombley, who he owned and kept under lock and key. (Two weeks later I stole this pilot away from him and you could hear old Hank howling all the way to Wacker Drive.)

Trombley run her in circles one way and then the other and he backed and he came ahead and I hadn't had any lunch or supper just 4,000 drinks with my friends from St. Paul. Finally we saw the searchlight of the towboat way downriver and in about an hour of horsing around we met her down at Jacqueline Light and took a load off her and she went upriver. Well, Trombley had picked up this loaded barge off the head of the tow facing downstream so it took one half hour to get it turned around during which the head got stuck in the mud by the railroad yards.

"How does she lift her stern, Cap?" says Hank Miller. "Does she answer those fine backing rudders?"

"Tell that useless deckhand to bring up a cup of coffee," says the pilot, Captain T. Trombley, himself.

"We didn't put no supplies aboard yet," says the shore boss.

We got up to the drawbridge and blew the whistle but nothing happened so we laid in the stream for a while and pretty soon a 300-car Great Western freight train came out of the East Dubuque tunnel and begun to creep across the bridge at 1 m.p.h. The engine got across and the engineer was so tired from this effort that he stopped the engine by the old shot tower and took a short nap while the caboose was still over in Illinois down by the Frentress barn or Coyle's Cabin Camp someplace. He finally dragged his string off the bridge so we blew again but this time an Illinois Central freight with 400 cars came out from behind the shot tower and onto the bridge from Iowa and crawled across and into the tunnel and when it got out of the tunnel in East Dubuque the engineer stopped the engine, with his string of cars clear through the tunnel, across the bridge, through town, and the caboose up the Catfish Creek valley near Rockdale. We waited while the engineer went over to Petry's tavern and had a beer and shot the breeze for a while with Charlie Naylor the bartender. While he was doing this the conductor, who was in the caboose, went up to the store in Rockdale and bought himself a Snickers bar and a White Owl cigar.

"No coffee," says the pilot. "What you planning to do with that fifty thousand dollar galley, hire it out for parties?"

We got through the bridge and delivered that load to Interstate.

"When and the hell are they going to dredge this place?" says ole Cap Trombley. "There ain't enough water in here to spot my grandmother."

So he put her in the mud about fifteen feet off the pilings and while the deckhand was trying to fish the tie-up lines off the pilings with the spike pole he fell into the river.

We fished him out and turned loose of the load and went up to the other end of the tipple to pick up the empty. There wasn't enough water up there to get in behind the empty barge so we yanked it out on a line and got faced up with plenty of advice from the congregation in the pilot house, most of whom had never seen a barge pickup in their lives.

The Big Barge Despatcher up in the sky had ordained that this barge was to be a barge with the hatch covers all piled up in a stack at each end. This meant that from the pilot house you couldn't see the river at all, only just a wall of hatch covers.

Coffeeless Cap Trombley worked her out to the channel

and they opened the bridge and Vernon the deckhand climbed up on top of the hatch covers on one side and I climbed up on the other side to give the pilot signals and help him through the draw. Vernon was wandering around on his side in the glare of the searchlight making a lot of fancy hand signals like he was directing traffic at Eighth and Main Street and dancing around and I saw what was going to happen and I hollered "Look out, Vernon!" but it was too late he fell off those hatch covers backwards and lit on the deck of the barge and broke his leg.

"His leg is broke," the "Port Captain" hollers up to the pilot house after we had looked him over.

"Too bad he didn't fall on his head," Trombley roars back, "and he would of been all right."

And he was so fussed up by this occurrence that he hauled ass out of there, went upriver, turned her around and *backed* down through the bridge.

"How does she handle, Cap?" says Hank Miller.

"Maybe if I land her on the bridge pier," he replies, "I could get a cup of coffee off of the bridge-tender."

We got rid of that empty and went over to the levee light boat and the ambulance came and took Vernon away and we tied up and I went up to my brother's house. The last time I had had any solid food was an airline breakfast between New York and Chicago. And it was now 1 AM.

"I don't suppose you want anything to eat," says my sister-in-law. "I know all about how you just eat all the time on those towboats."

That's not all.

Vernon was still in the hospital with his broken leg and I had a date with Dr. Donald Conzett the next day to do some crewel work on my patent repeating hernia. The day after the operation Vernon's young brother showed up picking his teeth.

"How ya goin Cap?" he said.

"Lousy. I ain't goin," I said.

"Guess who's down the hall in bed?" he said.

"You tell me and then we'll both know."

"Trombley. He's in the same room with Vernon. Captain T. Trombley himself, master pilot."

"What's Vernon doin in the hospital with only a broken leg?"

"They might have to set it again or somethin."

"What the hell happened to Trombley?"

"Well see his driveway is on a slant like and he forgets to set the brake and his car runs over him."

"What about the boat?"

"They talked young Huggins into runnin her. He is doin all right but he backed onto some rocks in the harbor acrost from the Coast Guard and done some damage or ruther to the rudders. Say I didn't know there was no rock pile in there did you?"

"As a matter of fact I think even my mother knows there is rocks in there. Isn't young Huggins the one who knocked the pilot house off the *Resolute* over in Joliet?"

"Well, he was the oney one they could get. These here pilots don't grow in the bean patch along with the beans," he said, spitting in the wastebasket.

"There ain't no drydock to look at them rudders closer than St. Paul that I ever heard of," he said. "Well, I guess I will go down and jolly up Trombley and Vernon for a while."

So that's a rough idea of the first week of operations of

the Bissell Towing and Transport Co., incorporated in the State of New York.

We operated the *Coal Queen* for ten years and I was a "shipowner" and we all had fun. I really had more fun than troubles, but trouble and misery make better copy, just look at the front page of the *Times* any day. Or the Bellevue *Bugle* for that matter. Each year the cost of the insurance just about wiped out our profit. There were also a number of irregularities going on which make for comical reading now, but indicate in retrospect a Top Management Pattern fashioned by Gilbert and Sullivan.

It was supposed to be a "dinner bucket" boat. That is, the crew of two was supposed to bring their own grub in a dinner pail. However, in my absence, which was more than three quarters of the time, food purchasing for the boat crept into the picture. Not only that but it seemed that Captain Trombley, his deckhand, and the port captain were very fond of *shrimp cocktail*.

More coming.

We had a regular enamelware steamboat coffeepot and a two-burner bottle gas stove in the galley, but this didn't meet with Trombley's standards so he bought (*I* bought, that is, unbeknownst to me) an electric coffeepot so he could plug it in in the pilot house and personally supervise this very important part of the towing operation himself. Next we have the edifying spectacle, worthy of the Pentagon, of a towboat operating during all the daylight hours when no electricity was needed, with a 15,000 watt Kohler diesel generator going full blast for the sole purpose of running a coffeepot!

On my houseboat I had an air conditioning window unit. Sure, you're absolutely right: as soon as I was out of town

Trombley moved *that* up into the pilot house of the *Queen*.

Molo Sand and Gravel Co. also had a little towboat, right across the harbor from our landing, called the *Mary*. (They say this was not named for a female member of the family but for Our Lady of Sorrows.) Trombley was always trying to prove to the captain of the *Mary* that he had a better deal and that with *his* boss the sky and outer space were the only limits.

So now he could really lord it over the *Mary*, for he had an air-conditioned pilot house and an electric coffeepot, and he and the deckhand slurped shrimp cocktails between picking up and dropping coal barges.

This is no way to run a barge line. And I have no one to blame but myself. The only way to run an outfit like this is to take off your coat and run it yourself.

We finally had a race with the *Mary* and she beat us by a quarter of a mile over a five mile course. Admittedly we had so many guests and members of the family aboard for the event that water was lapping at the engine room door. Still, it was a defeat from which Captain Trombley never really recovered. And he made his last crossing not so long afterwards.

After he was gone I wished he was back, for he was a conscientious and excellent pilot, kept the boat up like a yacht, and never had an accident. If I could have got him back I would have supplied him with pilot house color TV and shrimp de Jonghe.

The rest is a history of bent rudders, landing accidents, busted pilings and damage claims. If you want an exercise that is guaranteed to land you in the giggle house in no time, just spend a few months trying to pry some cash money out of a marine insurance company. Let me tell you something friends, they are real happy to see those premium checks rolling in, but when it comes time to send some claim money out to the customers, the check-writing machine is broke down and anyway, they can't find an envelope and a stamp anyplace in the whole god damn office.

We staggered along for a few more years. My family and I had fun with the boat and used to take it off on wonderful weekends pushing my giant all-steel houseboat *No Bottom*. But as a commercial venture it was showing a good deal of weakness on the New York Stock Exchange; and the *Wall Street Journal* intimated that "on balance" its growth prospects were sagging.

At this juncture our latest captain failed to check the lubricating oil in my beautiful, lovely Caterpillar engines. The results were not quite fatal but I took it as an omen of worse things to come.

I sold the *Coal Queen* to a river man who has more sense than I. He and his son run it themselves on a strictly no-shrimp basis.

THIRTEEN

And It Was All So Unnecessary

1938.

Married! Settled down! AAAAGH! Help!

My, my, it was dreadful after knocking about Naples and drinking wine with the second engineer at Righi at the top of the incline railroad; stewing about in the stews of Port Said, a willing ingredient; potted in Piraeus; stewed, screwed and tattooed in Marseilles.

"What's that light off to starboard, Chips?"

"That's Elba. That's the island of Elba, son."

Well, no more of that.

The frightening thing about it was the finality of it all. ". . . til death do us part," the Reverend Jones, Episcopal, said, which meant there was no way out, now. Nice people, especially the royal family of Bissell, didn't get divorces. And there was My Job. My number was 17 on a big round time clock that we all punched four times a day down at the office and the office was all black fumed oak and Father had been there from 8 until 5 PM every day except Sunday since 1901!!! Fairly put me in a cold sweat that notion did. It never occurred to me that there would ever be any possible way of escaping from that time clock. According to Father's lexicon people who started on a job and didn't stay at it for 50 years were "quitters." If you stayed 20 years and then shifted to more congenial work you were a "drifter."

My plump jolly beautiful Boston bride had been somewhat reluctantly admitted to the exalted Bissellian ranks. Like an actress who stumbles over new lines she doesn't like, Mother could never seem to pronounce my wife's maiden name quite correctly. The Boston and New England background* was highly acceptable bridge-table fodder but the name was only a few years away from Schleswig-Holstein. Besides, we were too young. We should wait, say about ten years. T.S., there, Mother. On a salary of $22.50 a week, she eighteen, I twenty-three, we got married and went into digs.

We lived in a cellar. We had a five-room Belloc-Lowndes basement barracks with exposed conduit pipes in the ceiling, green moss in the kitchen sink, and a human body bricked up in the parlor wall. For this we paid $35 a month. My brother Mycroft dubbed it "The Cave." We were happy here and had lovely loud parties with live saxophones and on New Year's Eve John Roshek knocked over the Christmas tree. "White Swan" gin was $3.30 a gallon and on Thursday nights two adults could get into the State movie house for 19 cents and see a George O'Brien movie.

But it *was* a Cave, and one of those dark places that no cutesying up could really fix. The only radiance in it was our Youth and the euphoria of Being Married. We could lock ourselves in and lie entangled on the couch and nobody could say a word. No one would rap a shoe on the ceiling overhead and no one would come to the head of the stairs and say "Marian do you know what time it is? You have school to-

---

* Both of my wife's parents were actually born and raised up in Davenport, Iowa, 108 miles down the river from Dubuque and 173 miles up the river from Hannibal.

morrow you know." But it really was a Cave. We wanted something less dank. On $22.50 a week.

Spring came and I introduced Marian-of-the-Couch to the harbor and to the Mississippi River. In a leaky rowboat which was all I had but she didn't care even if she was from Pinckney Street — she liked it right from the beginning which was a lucky thing. She liked the willow bats and the greasy old boathouses and the riprap and those limestone bluffs. But the most surprising was that this land-bound New England child immediately contracted my own lifelong passion for "messing around in boats." English people are particularly addicted to this pastime and Kenneth Grahame has given us the classic eulogy on the subject in his lovely, watery, rivery, *The Wind in the Willows*.

"Nice, it's the *only* thing," said the Water Rat solemnly as he leant forward for his stroke. "Believe me, my young friend, there is *nothing* — absolutely nothing — half so much worth doing as simply messing about in boats. Simply messing," he went on dreamily: "messing — about — in — boats — messing —"

"Look ahead, Rat," cried the Mole suddenly.

It was too late. The boat had struck the bank full tilt. The dreamer, the joyous oarsman, lay on his back at the bottom of the boat, his heels in the air.

"— about in boats — or *with* boats," the Rat went on composedly picking himself up with a pleasant laugh. "In or out of 'em, it doesn't matter. Nothing seems really to matter, that's the charm of it . . ."

At that time the lock and dam at Eagle Point was nearly finished but not operative. The river above the dam now wound its age-old course through a stricken bottomland wilderness of stumps; the trees had all been cut by the Corps of Engineers' contractors to provide, when the dam was closed, miles and miles of underwater stumpfields to snatch the bottoms out of flatboats and bend propellers into artistic non-propulsive shapes. Ecology had not become popular then — Joe Penner was still trying to sell his duck and we were innocent. Today any suggestion of such wholesale devastation would be greeted with widespread air pollution in the form of Ecology Screams and there would be no nine-foot channel on the Upper Mississippi.

Up into this graveyard of trees we blundered in our rowboat, and we found two very large floating cottonwood logs left behind by the Corps of Engineers and their handy helpers. We tied them up to a stump and went home to the Cave, for it was growing dark.

One of the great things about marriage is Getting Away from Mother's Cooking, or in my case, Mother's 5-dollar-a-week Hired Girl's Cooking. This is an un-American sentiment but deeply felt. Mom's apple pie is oft times pasteboardy and mucilaginous. No longer did I have to eat bread pudding, rice boiled for an hour and a half, lamb chops like anthracite clinkers, bumpy mashed potatoes, a "nice custard" leaking water at the seams.

My absolutely legal wife rattled them pots and pans and presently we sat down to an escaped con's meal of chili con carne with Krispy Krackers, Italian spaghetti, cream style corn, hot biscuits, chicken gravy, side order of pork chops, bread and butter pickles, A-1 sauce, green Jello, Mallomars and Fig Newtons with Doctor Pepper. That was being married. No more Mother's choices. Lovely lovely.

"What are we going to do with those big logs?" She asked me.

"I guess we had better make a raft," I said.

Finding boards and such was no problem on the islands then. All I took was a hammer and a saw and some nails on a Saturday morning and by noon we had a pretty fine raft. Meanwhile She had been scouring around amid the ruins of a former riverside cottage and she brought back two *rocking chairs* for raft furniture. I set up a jackstaff with a rag tied onto it. We made a sweep out of an old washboard nailed to a pole. We also of course had the rowboat and the oars. We turned loose. We worked her out into the stream.

A raft on a lake or a pond is fun but it is work making it go anyplace. Arafting on a river is all pleasure, all funny, you just do nothing and the town begins to move past and pretty soon Illinois and Wisconsin are both moving like a panorama. It's a free ride and people in boats come along and they lay alongside and they say, "What are you people doing setting in them rocking chairs in the middle of the river?"

First off we went through the open lock chamber of Lock 11, Mile 583. This was a historic passage for both us and the lock. It was the first time we had ever been through a wide open lock chamber on rocking chairs and it was the first and last raft ever to go through Lock #11 on the Nine Foot Channel Project.

"Now I've seen everything," is what the government idlers standing around would have said except that this tedious expression had not yet been invented. Instead they said "Christ, he's got a jane with him and they're settin on rockin chairs."

We tied the raft up in Seventh Street Slough that evening and went home to another meal of things I could never get, or was not allowed to eat, under the parental shingles. Like knockwurst and sauerkraut. Like corned beef and cabbage.

Seventh Street Slough is a mess now, like the rest of Dubuque, but then it was an interesting place. For one thing there was a genial squatter there named Mr. Steele, who lived in a shanty boat pulled out of the water and jacked up under the huge friendly cottonwood trees. Mr. Steele knitted fish nets and did lots of interesting things. He kept raccoons in neat clean cages and hound dogs on chains, and the place was sort of littered with bantam hens and roosters, pea fowl, and a few resplendent Hamburg chickens.

This spot has been improved into an industrial no man's land now, and where the banty roosters once strutted the Virginia Carolina Chemical Co. has erected a fertilizer plant the size of the Dnepropetrovsk power house.

That weekend old Al of Winona-to-Hannibal fame showed up from foreign parts and we did another stretch of river on the raft. Old Al was an original member of the Catfish Creek boating and freight-hopping society, a writer of desperate tales of horror, mystery, and adventure, an H. G. Wells fan, and he could sing in a baritone chest voice all the verses of *"Die Beiden Grenadiere"* in German.* (*"Nach Frankreich zogen zwei Grenadiere/Die Waren in Russland gefangen . . ."*)

We packed a hamper — well, we threw some food and some bottles of Dubuque Star beer into a soup carton from Tenenboms — and we floated on the breast of Mother River slowly and delightfully, comfortably, smoothly, and with no expenditure of effort whatsoever, drifted at ease with bottled beer and potted meats past the old town and downstream into the watery wilderness of Cattese, Nine Mile Island, Tadymore River, The Hole in the Wall, Deadman's Crossing, Gordon's Ferry — skirting Harris Slough, Stone Slough, and gemlike Lake Lindecker — to arrive silently at sundown in the roadstead off Bellevue, its riverside globe-lights beckoning. We spent the night at the tiny Weck Hotel

---

* Robert Schumann (1810–1856). Written in 1840 with words by Heinrich Heine (1797–1856).

on the riverfront, owned by the formidable Weck sisters from Melbourne, Australia.

The next day after chocolate sodas for breakfast at Hodoval's drug store, Al departed by freight train for Dubuque. Paul arrived, chuckled and blinked for a while, and that day we drifted fifteen miles down past Harrington's Landing, Sand Prairie and Pomme de Terre Prairie, and the Savanna Proving Grounds ending up at sundown at Lainsville, Iowa. Lainsville is a trackside name board and that is all — it is just the place where that name board is. Why the railroads do this I can't say. One of my favorite towns in Wisconsin is Charme. This is a railroad shack beside the Burlington tracks below Bad Axe River with a big name board on it as though it was Omaha: CHARME.

We tied up our good old raft and said good bye and trudged down the Milwaukee tracks several hundred miles to Sabula from which, since this was before things all went to hell in the U.S.A., we had a *choice* of ways to get home via palace railway coaches gliding on ribbons of steel. Babies born today in Sabula or across the river in Savanna will spend their entire lives and die right in town without ever seeing even Clinton or East Moline if they wait for the train to take them away.

That was the end of rafting and I hope those rocking chairs are in use in some boarding house in Green Island or maybe the raft got loose and they floated all the way down to Le Claire, birthplace of William Frederick Cody (Feb. 26, 1846). (When going through Le Claire on route 67, stifling boredom can be easily avoided by *not following* any of the signs that say "Visit Buffalo Bill MUSEUM!)

Bill Burden had a houseboat. That may have started it. I mean our houseboat fever. He had a nifty houseboat with a screen porch and a wonderful kitchen and a McDonald force pump on deck to pump water into a tank on the roof. There was a plop-plop-into-the-river toilet and a Little Gem wood stove in the main cabin, and Aladdin mantle lamps. It was just about as snug as you could imagine. This was the first houseboat my child bride had ever seen and it was the first one I had ever been aboard that was not in the shanty boat class. This one had a design for living; design by the Boat and Boiler Works, the living provided by the occupants. Let me tell you that *everything you do* is more fun on a house-boat, even washing dishes. Pumping water is a party and stoking the fire, sweeping the deck, trimming the lamps are a lark when you can look out the parlor window and see a piece of driftwood go floating by with a bird riding on it.

So Bill and Lizzie used the houseboat for weekends and other type holidays and Bill was a chef and fed me my first roast coon, which coincided with my last roast coon. But oh how we loved that houseboat hardly anyone will ever know. The luxury houseboat boom is on now but the old *Pampoo* remains perfect in my memory, every rivery thing about it was simple and natural and gadget-free and right. The only houseboat that comes near is Mycroft's three-room *Hernando's* which he built with his bare hands and has gas lights. Duncan Glab had a nifty keen houseboat with a very entertaining electric generator but he decided to go straight, quit the river, and *joined the Golf Club*, the equivalent of Captain Ahab's abandoning the quest for the white whale and taking up with the Nantucket Croquet Association. Tom Roshek's houseboat *The Ark* was like a summer cottage afloat on a flood but it sank. Danny Fetgatter's houseboat was the biggest and most baroque but he hauled it ashore at Massey Station and jacked it up and it isn't a houseboat any more. Freddie Bissell built the only houseboat ever known to be the size of a telephone booth.

So how to get a houseboat? A houseboat we could *really live on* full time, forsaking the land utterly and floating, floating all day and all night in watery bliss together with the wedding presents, the bullterrier, and the upright piano. Months went by. There just weren't any houseboats to be had, that's all.

Except one day there *was* one.

It was advertised in the *Waterways Journal* and it was located at La Crosse, Wisconsin, 120 miles upriver. So we climbed into my 1935 Ford convertible sedan, which Mycroft called "The Trellis" because of the exposed top bows and fragments of tattered canvas formerly the top; listen, on $22.50 a week you can't buy new custom-made canvas auto tops; listen you kids of today, you don't know what we went through, why I never saw a ten cent piece until I was sixteen years old. And we drove to La Crosse and saw George Neilter who was living in a nice warm (it was March) cozy houseboat right below the railroad bridge. He rowed us across the river and there stranded on the island among the bare wintry trees was the former Corps of Engineers Quarterboat No. 237, looking for all the world like a frame country hotel transplanted to a barge. Two stories high, with a gable roof, overhanging Swiss balconies at each end, with *forty* twelve-light windows, it was an awesome sight. It was also sunk. The front door was open and the current, nearly up to the doorknob, was entering enthusiastically and rushing through the house and out the back door, *sixty feet away*. Yes, the barge was eighty feet long and that's quite a barge.

"Well that there leak now that don't amount to much," George said. "I will borrow this big fire pump from the city and pump her out and I will lend you that there pump until you get her down there to Dubuque."

We paid $500 for this monstrous leaker and $100 to a fisherman who towed it to Dubuque with a flatboat, us dangling behind on a line. The only time he said he could do it was at night and he had never been below Lynxville so he spent the night hunting buoys with a five cell flashlight while we were back on the house keeping her afloat with that City of La Crosse fire pump. This had a four-inch discharge and a big delivery but even so our new home had to be pumped every hour or it would have been The End. It was not really a fun trip but we made it to Dubuque harbor. Other pumps were brought into play and daily life became a struggle to keep our $500 investment and home from slipping beneath the waves. A sunken boat is the saddest sight on earth.

Mother had turned to stone since the announcement that we were going to live on a houseboat in that awful harbor or on that awful river. Her role of royalty incognito was fearfully threatened. She put Father in the Iron Maiden over night and gave him two days of the Chinese Water Torture combined with the Silent Treatment and Mutton Hash for both lunch and dinner. Then she turned him loose on me.

"Close the door," was the first piece of business at the office the next day and the second piece was "I don't want to hear any more of this nonsense about a houseboat. Your mother . . ."

"It's too late, Dad," I said. "The houseboat is in the harbor. I already bought it."

Ever since I had "grown up," I made Father nervous. Just being alone together embarrassed us both. Father got red in the face. It was a strange relationship: Father was afraid of Mycroft, I was afraid of Father. I made Father very nervous because I was "that crazy kid" who was always doing terrible muckerish things like doing things with girls, hiding *Paris Nights* magazine in the root cellar, and putting Stacomb on his hair. When he got all fussed up with me, with the door closed, he always said too much, usually something rude. In a panic, I fended this off by being facetious. It was a very bad scenario.

"You know what this will do to your mother, don't you?" he said.

Fortunately the phone rang before I had time to reply to that one. It was Ira Davenport, then president of the Boat and Boiler Works.

"Fred," he said, "I don't want that boy of yours to take that little wife of his to live on that quarterboat. Mackert says it's leaking like a sieve. I'm putting a whole new hull on that boat and I'm doing it at cost."

"What did you do," Father said after he hung up, "tell Ira Davenport you were a pauper?"

Mother and Father never *did* get any enjoyment out of "Dick Bissell's Houseboat" even though it soon became famous. Feature stories and pictures appeared in all the leading journals, and Mother even came to tea once with Hallie Lusch and Nina Day but Mother and Dad never got any *fun* out of it. They were the only people within a large radius who didn't.

What the shipwrights at the Boat and Boiler Works did is something that you probably could not get done at all today. Because the age of wooden-ship construction is over and the carpenters are fading away. What they did after they pulled this big barge-with-a-house-on-it out and jacked it up was to saw both gunwales off the barge for the full length of 80 feet. Then they made an entire new gunwale of timbers six inches thick built up to three feet wide and pinned together with drift pins. They jacked this up and just like cabinet work it slid into place a perfect fit, no planing, shaving, pounding, or cussing. "You can't get that kind of work no more."

While this was going on and I was up at the factory giving fairly unconvincing imitations of a Rising Young Executive, my old lady, who had now reached nineteen, was down inside the barge with a hoe and a shovel removing a six-inch deposit of smelly mud, sand, and goop, shoving it through holes in the bottom made by knocking out every tenth bottom plank. At the present time if you want a houseboat you go to a marina and buy a houseboat. The last one I looked at was about one quarter the size of the *Prairie Belle* and cost $22,250. We paid $500 for ours and Ira Davenport's bill for labor and lumber was $1,200. Even in 1939 that was CHEAP.

ON THE MAIN DECK

Living room with four windows. Baseburner.
Music room with full size piano.
Bedroom with four poster bed.
Bathroom with full tub.
Kitchen — very large.
Pantry number one. Large.
Pantry number two. Larger.
Kitchen deck 8′ x 19′.

ON THE SECOND DECK

Two bedrooms.
Sewing room.
Tank room.
Enormous fun room with full-width balcony.

Now you take one of the new houseboats that "sleep eight." Well, you know that means eight people can lie down somehow and get through the night. After one gay weekend as guests the wives will think of really outlandish excuses to get out of a repeat.

There's no room for real comfort on any conventional factory-built luxury cruiser, or sailboat either, until you get into the yacht class; and this is no fun either because all large yachts are owned by people who say things like "Bimini" and "Pipe yourself aboard and we'll buy you a (a) snort (b) drinkie (c) grog (d) martooni."

We had no cocktail flag on the *Prairie Belle* but plenty of room. We were just as comfortable as in a house. We didn't have bunks — we slept in a four-poster bed.

We lived there. That's what, I guess, had congealed Mother.

We had no other home. Everything we owned was in this boat, afloat on the Mississippi.

I worked in an office — I walked home to a houseboat. We invited people to dinner — they came — to a houseboat. We called for the doctor — he arrived — at a houseboat. The milkman came — to a houseboat. The piano tuner and the piano teacher both came down to "that awful harbor" — to a houseboat. We went to Chicago — and came home — to a lovely welcoming houseboat with a beautiful range boiler and *mit vielfarbigen bunten Gemutlichkeit* and steamboats out the window and oil lamps swinging gently from the ceiling.

The paperboy hurled the evening paper — it lit with a thump on the deck — of a houseboat. The dog came home from the vet — to a houseboat. We basted the Thanksgiving turkey — on a houseboat and came home from church to a houseboat. There was no other place to go. It was our home, our only home in the day and in the night, on long summer days when the river sparkled in the South wind and on winter nights at thirty below when the contracting ice made pistol shots in the hull.

We brought the Christmas tree home — across the tracks and down the bank — to the houseboat — and we put a wreath on the door — of the houseboat *Prairie Belle* at Mile 580 on the Upper Mississippi. We went to the Grand Ballroom of the Julien Hotel to the Christmas dances and friends came down afterwards, the girls in their glacier satin gowns and the men in their dress suits — to the houseboat in the harbor. At one AM Mycroft in white tie and tail coat was cutting figures on the harbor ice outside the kitchen windows. Good friends were singing around the piano. The bullterrier, the white cavalier, was lying in front of the parlor stove and the cat was in her corner. Everybody was young and everybody was beautiful . . .

Good God can it be thirty-three years ago?

I was out at the farm to see Mother the other day. Dad has been gone for years but Mother is still out there on the old place, in her new tweed suit. Mother is now ninety-three years old.

We were in the parlor and I was looking out the bay window and beyond the two oak trees toward Rockdale. A pretty vista. So far the spoilers haven't got it but it's only a question of time. Mother was rambling on.

". . . and it was all so unnecessary," she was saying.

"Sorry," I said. "What was unnecessary, Mother?"

"Richard," she said, "why did you have to go and live on that houseboat?"

FOURTEEN

But the License Bug Has Bit
and Wounded Me

The War came to bust up my houseboat idyll. It busted up everything as a matter of fact. The prevailing notion amongst most of my friends was that it was spoiling their fun and would probably cost them a good deal of money in the long run. Everybody listened to the radio a lot and somebody punched somebody else at Freddie Leiser's bar in East Dubuque — something about F.D.R., or Harry Hopkins and Churchill, or what "Eleanor" said about Pearl Harbor.

It was time to go someplace.

I personally blame the Japanese for terminating my youthful dream-days afloat and for my loss of the finest houseboat on the Upper Mississippi — that Blackstone, that Ambassador East of houseboats. On the other hand, but for the day of infamy near Pearl City, I would not have a pilot's license with a steel engraving on it and a lot of important signatures and framed under glass like you see in the corridors of the boats of the Washington State ferry system.

I never expected to go up for license of any kind when I

went over to Joliet on the canal and joined up with the Central Barge Co. All I expected was just to be a deckhand and do my work and have no worries; everybody on a towboat has something to worry about, even the striker engineer, except the deckhands. If he had stayed in the forecastle Lord Jim would not have had all those head complaints and going from one shrink to another.

Besides, licensed pilots were actually a race apart. How did they get that way? It was all very mysterious. There were, for one thing, very few of them. Also very few licensed mates and licensed engineers, for the very simple reason that there were not, back then, an awful lot of boats on the Upper Mississippi. It took years to get a license and who knew whether you'd get steady work? Steamboat captains and pilots — well it just took something, to go through all that, that most people didn't have.

Anybody back then who could make an X on a piece of paper could graduate from the state university at Iowa City. This made a person a "college grad" and carried with it the privilege of speaking farmer dialect forever more; it also absolved one from ever reading another book of any kind until the Huebsch-Ris master of ceremonies put a lily in one's hand. It was assumed for a long while there, that being a "college grad" also carried "Success" with it, and trips to Chicago, the Bismark Hotel, party girls, and Phil Cavaretta at Wrigley Field. Many lives west of the water tower faded like the hall carpet while waiting for it to happen.

But getting a pilot's license was all alien and queer and *difficult*. For example to do it you had to *live on a boat*. And go away far away on that boat. And *stay* on that boat or another boat. And *work* on those boats. Out of doors on those dirty barges. And half the time after dark! At night. And live with crude men who had no Lodge Night and no Bowling Night. A person would have to be kinda crazy to do like that wouldn't he?

I took the Burlington Twin Cities *Zephyr* from East Dubuque to Aurora. (The *Zephyr* was as life-giving and eternal as the sun, but it is gone.) Aurora to Joliet on the bus and with quavery emotions down to the canal and into the old quarterboat, which was the local office of the Central Barge Co. of Chicago.

Captain Connie Ingersoll, Jr., himself interviewed me. He had been on the deep water and the seven seas as a deck officer and he was a pistol.

"I see from this application you were on the *James W. Good*. Who was on her?"

Didn't he *believe* I had been on her? Or what?

"Louis Nyhammer was captain," I said, "and Morris Burge was pilot, and we had a radio operator named Woods. Don Mullady was mate and Blackie Crist was watchman* and for deckhands we had Richard Nyhammer, Whitey Henkel, Bob Freyhage, Jud Mullady, a guy named Moxie, an old man named Larry from Minnesota, and a boy from off a farm near New Vienna, Iowa . . ."

"O.K., O.K.," he said.

". . . and I don't remember the cook but the maid was a real pretty girl from Cassville, Wisconsin."

"O.K., O.K.," he said. "Upper Mississippi I suppose?"

"St. Louis to St. Paul. Once in a while we went up the St. Croix with a barge of sisal for the penitentiary at Stillwater."

"It says here you were on the American Export Line as ordinary, that right?"

"On the *Exochorda*," I said. Well, I wonder if he believes

---

* On the river "watchman" is often used instead of second mate.

me and what the hell difference does it make, I only want a deckhand's job.

"Who was on her then?" he said.

"The only officers I knew were Mr. Kelly and Mr. Fayle. Frank Pickard was bosun. And Jack Ziereis was on there, they called him 'Bananas.' He was sort of famous."

"So you shipped with 'Bananas' did you?" he said. "He was on the Grace Line with me."

"Yes, to the Black Sea."

"How soon can you go up for mate's license?"

"Oh I don't want license and all that."

"Yes you do," he said and it was an order.

"Well I can't go up for license for over a year anyway," I said.

"How do you open a new coil of line?" he said.

"Pull the outside end up through the hole in the middle," I said.

"You can start on the *Shepard*," he said.

"Thanks," I said.

"Don't forget," he said. "You're going up for license. *You* want it, you understand. You're not some country boy, you want license."

What this was all about was that *they* wanted me to get a license. Practically none of their mates had licenses — well, very few. In the first place, although there was no regulation about it, it looked better all around to have licensed personnel. If there was an inquiry about an accident before the Steamboat Inspectors, for example, it looked a lot better if you were giving testimony as a licensed man. But the main reason was because they had built this gigantic steamboat, the *Alexander Mackenzie*, and on a steamboat they were required to have two licensed mates at all times. Now mates on the river have a way of walking away sometimes and getting lost. They *had* to have a supply of licensed mates and pilots and engineers to keep her wheel turning. All their other tow-boats were diesel boats which require no licensed men at all.

Most of the mates on the barge lines were farm boys who had decked long enough to know the work and become mates. They weren't necessarily any good at it, and most of them were scared to death of the idea of going up before the Inspectors and answering a lot of questions and *writing an examination*. A lot of them couldn't hardly write a letter home. And some of them didn't even like to go into the pilot house with a cup of coffee they were so aware of their lowly station, much less go into a Steamboat Inspector's office. "United States Local Inspectors, Steamboat Inspection Service." They just could not ever open a door any possible way with those words on the glass. That's why all the deckhands weren't plugging for license. Damn few of them.

On the barge lines the mate is like a foreman — only on the river, on the Central Barge Co. anyway, he worked right alongside the men out on deck, making tow and locks and all except painting and soogeeing and chipping and cleaning out bilges and sweeping barges and wheeling coal and carrying bucket planks and standing a timberhead watch on a barge tied off in the rain and miserable jobs like that. Some of the mates even did these things too, if they happened to feel like it. I have to tell you some of these deckhands-turned-mate were miserable. They wanted the extra wages and the mate's cabin, and the title sounded good around the saloon or at home but they didn't like to order their former buddies around and responsibility made them nervous — all they really wanted was to be deckhands and told what to do. Besides, half of the ass-eatins and chewin-outs from the pilot house lit on the mates, not on the deckhands. It was small consolation for a mate to be able to pass insult and injury on to three or four simple old boys in overhalls.

The *W. A. Shepard* was built in 1927 by the Charles Ward Engineering Co. in Nashville on the Cumberland River. She was originally owned by W. C. Kelly Barge Line and came out with Fairbanks-Morse diesels giving 720 hp. Later on she was re-powered with two National Superior 14½ x 18 8-cylinder diesels giving 1,350 hp. Central Barge bought her from the American Barge Line Co. in 1938. She had a very high pilot house built on top of the original pilot house. Her hull set low in the water and she had very high twin stacks. Some thought her a freak but she had an old-time steamboaty look to her that I admired. (She had a big sister, or brother, built in 1925, called the *George T. Price*.)

This towboat became a home to me, both on the Illinois River and on the beautiful Upper Mississippi River, and even in the dry dock at St. Louis Ship down at Jefferson Barracks.

You probably think that after all that interviewing I was being hired for a pretty nice job, lowly perhaps, but civilized. Perhaps I would be like the deckhands you have seen on the Cunard Line, polishing brass in their jumpers or turtle-neck jerseys and wearing the Jack Tar hat with *Parthia* in gold on the band. Not so bad.

What I was actually doing, for one hundred dollars a month, was selling myself into slavery on the coal barges of the Illinois River and the Chicago Drainage Canal. We slept in a pore white trash bunk room and worked alternate watches of six hours on and six hours off for forty days at a time. That was an 84 hour week and we worked Sundays and all holidays. There was not hardly any standing around or screwing the dog. This was at the hawser's end of the long

long period, since the beginning of time, when men who followed the water were expected to act like brutes and seamen
submitted to being treated like animals. Brutality was out
but certain traditions of the sea remained and one of them
was Making Work. Captains could not stand the sight of a
deckhand, on watch, sitting on a timberhead. It made the
blood rush to their heads and their teeth turn to iron. So on
the night watch we scrubbed and soogeed and wasted all
kinds of time and scraped bilges and did all sorts of goofy
repetitive unnecessary and disgusting jobs.

We had an old boy from Hickman, Kentucky, when I was
on the Lower Mississippi on the *Mackenzie* and he said:
"I see ole Mr. Captain acomin up the guard so I just picks
up that ole anvil in the deck room and holds it in my arms.
He seen I was astrainin on somethin and he was satisfied and
went away."

It was particularly bad on the Illinois River, which was
near to the home office and Big Shots might appear at any
time and find a deckhand sitting on a timberhead. Once we
got over to the Upper Mississippi, we still had to do foolish
chores at night, but not so much, especially if there was a
relief captain aboard. But it never let up.

A few years after I quit I was at home and Captain Gene
Woods called me up from downriver at Bellevue coming upstream and he asked me if I would like to go decking for old
times' sake as he was short a man.

It was a Sunday noon and after packing away fried
chicken and mashed spuds and hot biscuits and boysenberry
pie and a gallon of java I went out on deck with my gloves to
go to work; and the mate and the deckhands just all set
around smoking and lazing off. There were even *two* deckhands sitting on timberheads. And the captain could see
them from the pilot house, too. I just wondered how long

they would set there before lightning struck. We passed Finley's Landing, and nobody made a move, and we left Hurricane Island Light behind us; everybody still the same, rolling cigarettes, shooting the bum fodder, spitting in the river. It made me nervous so by the time we came up to the lower daymark below Waupeton I couldn't stand it any longer and I said "Say when do we set to work, ain't we going to do nothing?"

"Work? Why this here is *Sun*day. We don't do no work no more on *Sun*day."

"*Sun*day?" I said. "So what? Why, we use to work Sunday, Christmas Day and every day."

"You wasn't so smart. You didn't have no union, you dummy."

That's right, we didn't. But they've got one now and a crummy lousy deckhand gets 300 dollars a month, all he can eat, paid vacations, insurance, hospitalization, a gold watch for Christmas, and after two years a bonus of a Chevvy four-door sedan and two weeks in the Kahala Hilton.

Mycroft, my brother, used to say "What's all this talk about work? I never see anybody working on those boats going past town."

So I used to tell him about it but he never believed me, anyway. I guess he thought I wanted sympathy. I didn't want any goddam sympathy. I didn't have to stay on the barge line, none of us did. The fact is we *enjoyed* being the downtrodden of the earth. It gave us all a chance to show what we could do. Besides, a lot of the work was fun.

On the Illinois River we made up an eight barge tow at Havana, Illinois — hustling out on our backs about twenty 80-pound ratchets — steel cables — huge chain links — shackles — safety lines — lock lines . . . 48 hours later we delivered the loaded barges, in Joliet, dismantled the

entire rigging, turned loose and made up a new tow, of empties, carrying out about twenty 80-pound ratchets, etc. etc.
Going downstream with empties was faster, so in about 24
hours we would be back down at Havana again, strip the
rigging off the empties, and make up a tow of eight loads,
hustling out two tons of ratchets, chains, wires, shackles,
safety lines, lock lines. And this went on forever.

It was hard to get used to. About half the deckhands that
signed on didn't last very long. After a few trips, with the
mate breathing down their necks and all that constant
making tow, they would say, "I don't mind eatin shit but
when they start into feedin it to me with a coal scoop why
count me clear out," and when we got to Joliet they would
go up the bank.

The first month was the worst, same as at Stateville Prison
there in Joliet four miles away from the river.

After the first month I could pick up a ratchet without my
knees buckling like a Charlie Chase skit, and I was one of
the crew. Accepted.

I learned that there is something to be said for slavery
— no responsibility for one thing — and that freedom, so
highly touted, can have its disadvantages. I was the slave
but I was eating like a panther, sleeping like dead, and didn't
give a damn for nothing. The captain was supposed to have
won through to freedom from the deck, from wheeling coal;
but he wasn't free he was a slave to the company and he took
Pepto-Bismol.

Mark Twain learned the river from the pilot house. That's
the way they did it in those days. All the deck work was done
by Africans for about 10 cents a day. Everybody knows that
Sam Clemens paid Horace Bixby 500 dollars to learn him
the river between New Orleans and St. Louis. He was a cub

pilot and never so much as busted a fingernail working which shows he was a lot smarter than I am.

After several months of this ding-dong life on the Illinois River we were sent to the Upper Mississippi for an entire season, that is until she froze over in December. Whenever I think back to steamboating and my own life on the Mississippi I see myself on top of the pilot house of the *W. A. Shepard* on a beautiful summer morning up above Britts Landing and going through Coon Slough; I am polishing the searchlight, and the pilot is John Winslow, or maybe Norm Hillman, or big jolly Ricky, Ralph Richtman; the lotus are in bloom in the ponds beside the channel, and the white egrets are dabbling around; there we are, in the middle of the wide sunny valley, moving slowly up the river with our hopes and our youth, and our coal.

Aug. 10, 1942
Red Wing, Minn.
Upper Mississippi

. . . we had to drop a barge last night at Winona and what a mess. Took us two hours and a half — ran the whole head end aground, busted all the couplings and wires, then got off and right away ran aground again. Had to get out the yawl and carry lines ashore and tie up to a couple of cottonwood trees — pulled one tree down but got out from under in time — we got the tow put together again with about ten tons of new chains and ratchets and we are ready to turn loose but Oh No, Cap decides he wants them tie-off lines doubled up. So it was into the yawl again — me and Stevie, for another 45 mins. Send me some money to Alton for some gloves. I have sewed my present ones up so often there is no original stitching left. Well I will be going for my mate's license in about six months and I am going to do it and go for

pilot's license too — don't laugh I am really going for it. The Shepard *is becoming a god damn* home *and that is the best news I can tell you* . . .

The first stirrings of the obsession to "Get that License" are here seen in typical form. A few months later the fever had increased.

St. Paul, Dec. '42
M/V W. A. SHEPARD

. . . lock lines frozen to the deck and glare ice on the line decks. Tied up below Robert Street and here I am in the god damn sleet toting chains, while right up above us here at the top of the hill the sheiks are sitting around in the nice warm gin mills with real live girls who are wearing TANGEE lipstick. Well my turn will come. In the mean while we have 13 empties to butt all the way to far off St. Louis and they say Lake Pepin is making ice. All so I can go for mate's license and maybe some day pilot's license — it don't make good sense. Why do I want a pilot's license? Because it is Absolutely Unattainable. The license bug has bit and wounded me and I'm a goner.

In the winter of '42 the *Shepard* went back to the Illinois but Captain Ingersoll thought I should have some experience on a real steamboat so they sent me down to the Ohio River onto the *Mackenzie* running between Cincinnati and Baton Rouge and a few points in between including a number of sandbars. I was very glad to get out of the ice and sub-zero boating weather, even if it meant leaving my "home" and my buddies on the rattly old *Shepard:* Rusty, Scotty, Norm, Gene, Chuck, Frosty, Stevie, Paul, Joe, Stanley, Ironjaw . . . Life on the Lower Mississippi and Ohio was instructive but it would have to be your own native land for it to come up to the Upper Mississippi. We had plenty of exciting times and one big grounding on a falling river when we left barges high and dry, two of them to break their backs, down on the sand at Mark Twain Light below Memphis at Mile 259.0. And there was not as much joy on the *Mackenzie* either. The chief engineer was a passionate, particular, and glum individual who hated to go off watch and let someone else touch his engines. He viewed deckhands as belonging to one of the lower orders of primates and their presence in the engine room was strictly outlawed. The captain was a Gary Cooper type and worried a lot. He was glad to see me show up because I had learned the clerk job, taking care of all the paper work of which there was plenty, in addition to my job on deck. For this I received 50 cents a day, plus the privilege of sometimes doing the clerical stuff while my fellow deck-hands were out in the fuel flat in the rain. I also worked for Captain Steele as second cook for several weeks. This meant making Jello, listening to Joe Pierce the cook's complaints about his various marital mishaps, setting and waiting on the officers' table. This was one of those boats where you tiptoed into the pilot house with the coffee and got out in a hurry. There was no hanging around while the pilot kidded you for the benefit of whoever else happened to be there.

This captain was worried most of the time. It was one of the biggest sternwheelers in the country if not the world. The pilots were all trip pilots, not company men. One of them couldn't see too good. The river was in flood, we were double-tripping and hanging up and running out of fuel coal and Steele couldn't make no showing at all.

You can't take the exam for mate's license until you can show a certain number of years and months of service and get character letters from licensed officers. Some of the pilots and captains and engineers are pretty twitchy about giving character letters, the theory being that you are after their job. Some licensed people are just plain mean — like you find in every business everywhere. At any rate there is likely to be some hemming and hunking when you start asking for letters.

It was coming near my time off and I got a letter from Norm Hillman, master pilot, and one from Frosty Curts, chief engineer on the *Shepard*. But the one that really cut the souse with the Inspectors was from Captain Ralph Richtman, because he came from a long line of Upper Mississippi rivermen, from Fountain City, Wisconsin.

He was relief master pilot on the big old coal-burning wheel-splashing *Alexander Mackenzie*, and he came into my clerk's office and picked out this rough draft himself on the creaky old Remington:

CENTRAL BARGE COMPANY

Interoffice Correspondence

To Capt. Clifton Moffett and Capt. Hewitt Jones
    U.S. Local Steamboat Inspectors
    Post Office Bldg.
    Dubuque, Iowa

Gentlemen:

Richard Bissell will appear before you shortly to take an examination for the license of Mate on River Steamers. I have known Richard for the past year and have worked with him on the motor vessel WHEELOCK WHITNEY and on the steamer ALEXANDER MACKENZIE.

He has been with us on the MACKENZIE for the past three months and is still on here at present date, and I think that he is very capable, trustworthy and understands the work very thoroughly; at different times he has substituted for the watchman or second mate and his work has been very satisfactory at all times. And also I think that any one who can do the work satisfactorily on a boat as large as the steamer MACKENZIE and with tows as large as she handles is capable of holding a mate's license. I gladly recommend him for the license he now seeks.

Respectfully yours,

Ralph Richtman

Master and pilot
Str ALEXANDER MACKENZIE

FIFTEEN

Days as Free as Air, and Time
as Endless as the Sky

I t cost me one half of my month's wages to get home to
Dubuque on the day coach on my next time off, because
we were clear down in Natchez, Mississippi, when my time
came to go. This was a swell trip with the trains all jammed
to the vestibules with soldiers and soldiers' wives and soldiers' girl friends and all sorts of other people — during a
war everybody is all the time moving around. A girl from
East Feliciana parish, Louisiana, gave me her baby to hold
and bulldozed her way into the club car and was gone for
two hours. She came back with an old boy in tow with an
Adam's apple — she had him hanging on the ropes and at
Memphis he got off with her and the baby, although he
really was bound for Obion.

One of the best things about steamboating when you are
young, and not spavined, wore out and cynical, is getting
home to that girl who is waiting for you at the station all
dressed up like Tillie the Toiler, or in the kitchen in a cute
apron with a dab of baking powder on her cheek, or, in the
bedroom in those frilly black lacy doodads from that store
on Wabash Avenue in Chicago. Home is the sailor, home

from Natchez, from Vicksburg and Delta Point, home from the shifting sands of Issaquena County, Mississippi, and the dread bogs of the Yazoo River.

A couple of days later I went down to the post office building on Washington Park and went up to the third floor and looked at the door for a while. It said "Steamboat Inspection Service" and "U.S. Department of Commerce." I went out and walked around the park and looked at the stupid pigeons. It seemed strange, but only six years before I had been pacing up and down outside Peabody Hall in Cambridge, Massachusetts, in a similar state of panic. On that occasion the inquisitors were the entire faculty of the Harvard department of Anthropology and the event was my oral exam for my degree. As Ernest Hemingway would say, I outpunched them and knocked out Professor Ernest Hooton and gave Professor Alfred Marston Tozzer a black eye and showed them who was boss. Which made me, in due time, the only steamboat second cook on the entire Mississippi-Missouri-Ohio River system to be also a qualified and Licensed Anthropologist. None of this glory would do me any good now.

Finally I plugged up my courage and opened that door and went right into the "Steamboat Office."

Captain Moffett was waiting for me and he introduced me to Captain Jones. Both of them were old timers on the river and they knew everything and everybody that had anything to do with the river since 1903. Today the Coast Guard runs the show and the Officer In Charge could come from Portland, Maine, or Seattle and never have seen a Mississippi sandbar or a gar pike in his life. Captain Moffett and Captain Jones had been with the Army engineers, on snagboats, dredges, survey launches; they had known and worked for

Diamond Jo Reynolds and for the Streckfus family on their steamboats; they had known that old curmudgeon Captain Walter Blair personally; they not only knew the entire channel but had helped to put it in and they knew the history of the lights and who they were named for. They had helped to install the wing dams and had a personal historical interest in every buoy. They would say things like, "When we were dredging at Diamond Bluff in the summer of 1913 . . ."

The first thing they did was set me in a chair, put a steam syphon into me and begin pumping me out. They wanted to know who was second engineer on the *Mackenzie* and who were the trip pilots, and how did Richtman like it way down there on the lower river so far from Trempealeau and Molly, and did I know where George Heckman was at and whether we were doing much double tripping and did we ever go above North Bend on the Ohio. Then Jones said it was funny that a person with my, uh, advantages, was off decking on the steamboats. I said I liked it on the steamboats.

"What is this *Wheelock Whitney* in Ricky's letter I mean Captain Richtman's letter?" Captain Moffett wanted to know.

The company had just recently changed the name, from *W. A. Shepard*, and we had had to re-stencil the life rings and the yawl and the fire buckets and stuff like that with the new name: *Wheelock Whitney*.

I told him I thought Wheelock Whitney was some big cheese with Truax Traer Coal Co. in Chicago and Truax Traer must have a big interest in Central Barge Co. because they had boats called the *A. H. Truax* and the *Glenn Traer*. I said all I knew about Wheelock Whitney was that he went to Yale. This was the kind of inside stuff they liked, the big stuff.

"Yale," Jones said. "Think of that."

"Fred Bissell on the Planning and Zoning, is he your dad?"

I said yes.

"And you want a mate's license," Captain Moffett said. "Well, if that's what you want."

"That's what I want." I said.

"Say, is your brother the one that married that Adams girl?" Capt. Jones said.

I said that was right.

"I thought she married McDonald," Moffett says.

"No, McDonald married that girl from Kansas City. Her old man is a banker."

"Not the way I heard it. I heard he was a packer. I heard he was in the packing business."

"Could be," says Jones. "A lot of your big men are in lots of things. He could be in both your banking and your packing."

"Say do you know any of the Rosheks?" Jones asked me. "I bet you know Tom don't you?"

I thought of all the sweating I had been doing about this interview with THE INSPECTORS. Well, if *that's* what they wanted . . .

"Sure, I know Tom. I know all of 'em. Tom married Bissig. John married Preussner. Lenore married Ziepprecht."

"Wait a minute," the Senior Inspector said. "Which Ziepprecht?"

"Say, do you think the Rosheks own the store outright?" said Jones.

"Which Adams is that your brother married?" asked Moffett. "Is she iron foundry Adams or sash and door Adams?"

"No, no," said Jones. "She is sash and door Adams, am I right?" And I said he was right, she was sash and door.

Rowboat I built in the cellar in May, 1927,
when I was fourteen.

Boat we "lifted" at Winona.
I was sixteen.

A desperate character
on the Upper Mississippi.

Another desperado,
my buddy Al.

Bumming the freights,
Clinton, Iowa, to
Hannibal, Missouri,
1929.

On a slow freight
train through
Missouri.

Mother and Father,
1927. Mother in
stylish soup pot hat.

Mother and
"Richard," 1927.

Father, Mycroft and the author,
who is making a "funny face" to entertain Mycroft.

Ordinary seaman, New York to Mediterranean ports.
Our hero is front right.

Soldier of fortune on the Acropolis, Athens.

A skinny kid in the Merchant Marine, Alexandria, Egypt.
I am on left.

The mighty sternwheel steamer *James W. Good*,
from out on the barges, 1937.

Deck crew of the steamer *James W. Good*.
Deckhand Bissell second from left.

Newlyweds, 1938.

My eighteen-year-old New England bride, Marian van Patten Grilk, of Exeter, N.H., and Pinckney Street, Boston.

The WATERWAYS JOURNAL
EVERY WEEK

FIRST
SEPTEMBER
ISSUE

WEEKLY
SINCE
1887

Title Registered U. S. Patent Office No. 230-952

Vol. No. LII.   20 Cents a Copy   SAINT LOUIS, MISSOURI, SEPTEMBER 3, 1938 $3.50 Per Year   No. 23

AMERICAN BARGE LINE

Selects Superior

The American Barge Line Co., Inc., who transports freight from Pittsburgh to New Orleans and other points in the South, has these boats equipped with Superiors for propulsion and Superiors for auxiliary electric service.

With these economical engines, The American Barge Line makes a still stronger bid for supremacy in its field through assurance of faster service, increased pushing power and greater over-all efficiency . . . The Superior line of Marine Diesels is one of the most complete being manufactured in this country today. From this extensive line our Engineers will select the proper model and horse power to fit your particular power requirement.

No obligation is incurred by writing to our nearest office.

The "W. A. Shepard" and the sister ship "George T. Price", each is powered with a pair 800 horse power Superior Diesels.

THE NATIONAL SUPPLY COMPANY . . . SUPERIOR ENGINE DIVISION

FACTORIES: Springfield, Ohio; Philadelphia, Pa.   ·   SALES OFFICES: Springfield, Ohio; Philadelphia, Pa.; New York, N. Y.; Los Angeles, Calif.; Houston, Texas.

"The Riverman's Bible." *Waterways Journal*, September 3, 1938,
featuring the *W. A. Shepard*, later *Wheelock Whitney*.
She was a "morphidite" but I loved her.

Marian on deck of houseboat *Prairie Belle*.

Marian on deck of houseboat with government steamer *Wakerobin* in background. Dubuque harbor.

Deck and balcony of our houseboat-home, *Prairie Belle*,
moored in front of the Star Brewery across from East Dubuque, 1940.
Marian on deck of launch *Alert* alongside. Steamer *Patrick Hurley*
going through East Dubuque railroad drawbridge.

Intrepid second mate of the *Glenn Traer*
on the Illinois River, 1943.

The author as a river pilot.

Mark Twain as a river pilot.

The steamboat *Sailor* on the Monongahela.

My towboat *Coal Queen*, Dubuque, 1959.

With son Nat in flatboat *Cassville*.

PHOTOS BY HOWARD SWIFT, DES MOINES "REGISTER"

Sunday papers on
the Mississippi, 1962.

The treehouse. Nat,
Pop, Stasie, Sam.
The whole end of
this island and the
treehouse have since
disappeared.

PHOTO BY JOHN SZARKOWSKI

With daughter Anastasia
in houseboat *Floating Cave*, 1960.

PHOTO BY JOHN REYNOLDS, THE CEDAR RAPIDS "GAZETTE"

On deck of houseboat *No Bottom*, 1965.

PHOTO BY HOWARD SWIFT, DES MOINES "REGISTER"

Approaching *No Bottom*, at Schinkles Bar Island,
Mile 574.2, Upper Mississippi.

With Mother and Mycroft aboard excursion boat
at dedication of "Bissell Harbor."

"Well," says Moffett, "one of the foundry Adams's daughters married somebody pretty big."

"You're thinking of that Rose girl," I said. "She married one of the foundry Adamses."

"I thought that Rose girl married that Loetscher, the one that plays golf," Jones said.

"No, he married that Engel girl," I said.

"Then your brother's wife's sister's husband must be the one that owns that houseboat." And I said that was the one.

"Well then," he said, "he must be related to the Riders somehow or other."

"What Riders is that?" Moffett said. "The ones with Tri States Dredging?"

"No. Tri States is out of Green Bay," Jones said.

"Well then, how did they get to Dubuque?" Moffett said.

"They didn't have to get here," Jones said. "They been here all along I expect. Listen young man, tell me something else."

"I hope I have the answer," I said.

"Who did young Woodward marry?"

"Why let's see, he married Ziepprecht's cousin, she is . . ."

We eventually got down to my examination for mate's license except that first I had to get on the Burlington and go up to the Public Health doctor in La Crosse, Wisconsin, and have my color-blind test because there was no Public Health doctor in Dubuque. No, it doesn't make any sense as I look back on it, but that's what I did. It may have been that the eye doc in Dubuque wanted $5 for a color-blind test and the Public Health doc in La Crosse was free. So if the round trip fare to La Crosse was, say $4.10 I would save 90 cents. I don't doubt that's why I went. Days were as free as air, and time was as endless as the sky. But 90 cents was nearly a dollar.

Government organizations that I have known (and loved) have had a tendency toward rigidity. Resistance to changing conditions has at times been noted. Flexibility in modifying to revised technologies has ofttimes been wanting. Procedural formulations have become on occasion imprisoned in the dungeons of tradition.

The examination I took "To Mate of Inland Steam Vessels" had been conceived, tested, and frozen solid in the days of the packet boat. It took no notice of the fact that there were no "cargo vessels" on the Mississippi River either with or without passengers. The age of the high-powered, high-compression, low-cost, and low-color diesel-powered towboat manipulating barge fleets of huge tonnage had escaped their attention. I was asked questions about loading swine, stowing cotton bales, and sparring off.* When I took my pilot's license later on I was confronted with questions about possible quandaries in the pilot house resulting from a *sidewheel steamer breaking down on one side*. (Such is the devious ingenuity of a highly honed, razor-keen intelligence that I mastered this question easily although I had never been on a sidewheel steamer in my life.)

The examination went well enough. It took me about two days of writing. There were frequent breaks from *Vessels meeting at confluence of two rivers* to evaluate further the Dubuque social organism. Then it was back to stowage of case oil and rules governing *Vessels moored or anchored and engaged in laying cables or pipe, submarine construction, mat sinking, bank grading, dike construction, revetment, or other bank protection operations*. We finally got

---

* "Sparring off" is a technique for getting a boat off a sandbar which was last used in the second reign of Emperor Grover Cleveland.

the higher echelons of Dubuque society all straightened out and Captain Moffett said I had passed the examination and that I had given satisfactory evidence to the United States Local Inspectors, Steamboat Inspection Service, for the district of Dubuque, Iowa, that my knowledge experience and skill in lading cargo and in handling and stowage of freight was such that I could be entrusted to perform the duties of Mate upon Steam Vessels of all gross tons upon the waters of the Mississippi and Tributary Rivers and that I was thereby licensed to act as such for the term of five years from that date.

At the top of this Magna Carta or Rosetta Stone of my life is an engraving of the *Alexander Hamilton* or a sister-ship on her way past Haverstraw on the Hudson River. Little did I suspect that twenty-four years later I would be standing in the engine room of this same boat, eating an Eichler's hot dog as we passed Haverstraw.

Now that I had this license I used to do a lot of looking at it, but I wasn't so sure now all of a sudden that I wasn't actually pretty happy as a deckhand. So I returned to the *Mackenzie* incognito, so to speak, and went back decking and never let on that I had that steel engraving of the *Alexander Hamilton* in my suitcase.

But Ricky, Captain Richtman that is, he told on me, and since the company had just bought the doctor Mayo Brothers' old steamer *Minnesota* they hauled me off decking on the *Mack* and shipped me up as mate on the *Minnesota*. I already told you about that but not all.

She was at Joliet and a curiosity. She was a regular old sternwheeler with all the proper engine room smells and fizzling sounds and a doctor pump and coal-fired boilers, but she had many many deluxe extras. She had dozens and dozens of electric fans; she had a few tile bathrooms with beautiful hotel-style plumbing fixtures; she had large, curved, and beveled plate-glass windows at the forward end of the main cabin; all the staterooms had innerspring mattresses. It had actually been a high-class houseboat, a yacht, a floating luxury hotel. And we were using it for a towboat, to tow grain and pig iron on the Tennessee River! Like the famed clippers of the Horn that end up as hulks or coal barges in Hankow.

We had a lousy trip and a slow one, down the Illinois and Mississippi and up the Ohio — nursing two grain barges and three empties. Winslow, Captain John, had been roped into this job and he was pretty grumpy about it and glad to get to Paducah where his license ran out so he could get back up home in the North again. By that time I had already discovered that none of our rigging was any good for towing standard barges, which was what we were to be using up the Tennessee. Also, with an old time steamer like this of course the pilot house is set way back on the roof so when you are down making up tow, facing up, and all that, you *can't see the pilot house*, which like to drove me crazy.

The company figured they would simplify things and put as many Southerners on that boat as they could find. The first ones I ran onto were James Jess and Lee Roy Higginbotham, both of them from Guntersville, Alabama. They had never been on a boat before. That's the kind of deckhands I had on my Very First Mate's job. James had on white shoes and he wore a baseball cap that said O U KID on it.

"Boy, ain't you got any other shoes?" I said.

"James he always wears them white slippers," Lee Roy said.

The firemen came aboard drunk. One of the trip pilots was half blind. We had a lady cook with short skirts and dirty legs. I had to beat the mess boy with a club to get him to empty the garbage pails. We run aground, we hung up, we knocked down the stacks.

"Stop fussin," the old pilot would say. "Stop fussin, boy. You're twenty-nine years old. Now *I* have got somethin to fuss about. How would you like to be seventy-three years of age? Now that's no good at all. It's not right."

We laid at Sheffield, Alabama, and washed boilers while waiting for our pig iron to come by rail from Tuscumbia or some such place. There was a little gravel road that wound up through the trees to town. As you got up the draw aways a sidewalk appeared in the woods, and you followed this sidewalk like Dorothy, or Judy Garland, in Oz, and pretty soon houses began to appear and all of a sudden you were right downtown at the pool hall and the movie house. From there you could take a bus and bang across the river over to Florence and walk past the State Normal School in the evening and look in the windows and see the coeds studying.

We ran short a deckhand and they sent another one up from Guntersville. I never did find out why Guntersville, Alabama, was a bottomless labor market, which sent us, over the months, one hopelessly draggled case of ineptitude after another.

This new one was big and rather doughy.

"What's your name?"

"Roy B. Hopson. They mostly calls me Beehop."

"What you been working at, Beehop?"

"Making them doormats."

"What doormats?"

"Them doormats at the state pen."

"Are you clear out, or on parole?"

"On parole."

"You got any gloves?"

"No."

"Well you gotta have gloves on here. The wires and all will tear your hands all up."

"Well I ain't got any."

"Well go up town and get some."

"I ain't got no money."

Conversations like this were hanging in the air all over the valley, some of them dating back a hundred years or more. You could hear them in the chinquapin trees down by Widow Reynolds Bar and while double tripping Duck River Suck.

"You know this Beehop from down in Guntersville?" I asked Lee Roy later on.

"I guess I do. I guess everybody does. He's the meanest old boy in town."

"What did he do to get in the pen?"

"Why he shot and killed that man no reason at all right in front of the drug store. Sent him up for three years — ask me it should have been five — ten — keep him offn the streets."

"Three years eh? Well, I don't suppose it was a white man."

"White man? Oh hell no. Nothing like that."

The company gave up on it after a few months. They weren't making any money on it and the boat and the crew and the run and the accidents and the lady cook's dirty legs were more trouble to them than all the rest of the fleet combined.

I went back to the Illinois River as second mate on the *Glenn Traer* where I cut a very dashing figure in my black shirt and my mate's cap right out of the Cincinnati Regalia Co.'s catalogue.

SIXTEEN

Oblivious to Ontogeny

November 29, 1972
BY THEODORE SHABAD
Special to The New York Times

MOSCOW — Sometime last sum-
mer, as an unusual drought seared the
fields in the southern Ukraine, an African geology student from Nigeria and an
11-year-old flaxen-haired Moscow schoolboy were floating down the broad
Dnieper River on a raft.

What's this, a couple of afro-russky ecological organic
transcendental meditationists? I thought all the integrated,
youth-oriented back-to-nature environmentalists and candle-
makers were in the U.S.A. and Trafalgar Square. Why isn't
that flaxen-haired youth helping to flail the wheat and bletch
the new green corn of the glorious October Revolution with
his buxom flaxen-haired sister Svetlana Ivanovna? Not to
keep guessing, here's why:

Under the watchful eye of Georgi
N. Daneliya, at 42, one of the bright,
younger generation of Soviet movie di-

> rectors, the two were re-enacting a new
> screen version of a great American
> classic, Mark Twain's *The Adventures
> of Huckleberry Finn.*

All very thrilling I'm sure but I'll tell you one thing right off and that is, they have got the size of that raft all wrong, why the whole thing is about the size of a barn door. Now four people are supposed to be living on it and prancing around rehearsing the sword fight in *Richard III* and striking poses and going over their lines for *Romeo and Juliet* not to mention cooking, eating, getting at the jug, and raising hell. This Dnieper river version of Huck and Jim's raft is downright silly and the director, who claims to be "a Mark Twain fan since childhood," evidently can't read very good because he has got this sovietsky raft made of logs instead of *sawed lumber* like in the book: ". . . a little section of a lumber raft — nice pine planks . . ."

How do I know what this minute Slavic log boom looks like? Because they have got a picture of it in the *Times* right next to ads for *Young Winston*, *Cesar and Rosalie*, *Wild Appetites* and *Brothers and Lovers* ("a unique gay film. All male cast. Adults Only. Also very special Featurettes"). The African geologist seems to be steering with a clothesline pole, the Moscow schoolboy is standing lookout six feet away and the King ("a popular Moscow character actor") is sitting there between them in the middle of the Dnieper and looking very much like a popular Moscow character actor.

The hut appears to be made of reeds or pampas grass. It is just about big enough to accommodate an undeveloped serf of Singer midget size. The flaxy eleven-year-old is standing beside it so we have a scale. If the kid lies down in this teepee his feet will stick out, and if it rains he might just as well be outside.

Not that it matters to this producer or to any other producer, but actually the most famous raft in the world did not have a hut made out of sunflower stalks.

. . . so Jim took up some of the top planks of the raft and built a snug wigwam to get under in blazing weather and rainy, and to keep the things dry, Jim made a floor for the wigwam, and raised it a foot or more above the level of the raft, so now the blankets and all the traps was out of the reach of steamboat waves.

That's all clear enough. I am not picking on this Russian director exclusively — I am aiming at everybody who ever messes around with this story. Nobody pays no attention. They do a story about Athens and they think, "Oh well what difference does it make my superb direction is the main thing," so they make a set of the Parthenon that looks like the Corn Palace in Mitchell, South Dakota.

The size of the "wigwam" is also clearly stated.

"Right in the middle of the wigwam we made a layer of dirt about five or six inches deep with a frame around it for to hold it to its place. This was to build a fire on in sloppy weather or chilly."

In other words, the most famous hut in the world on the most famous raft in the world was made of pine planks, water tight, and big enough to contain a fireplace and also two full-size beds: a "straw tick" (Huck's) and a "corn-shuck tick" (Jim's).

The entire story is filled with perils of this kind and others far worse, and probably if it were done right it would still look wrong. I don't believe there is any possible way to do any form of dramatic treatment of *Huckleberry Finn* and have it "right." Attempts to dramatize the immortal saga, to fix, to adapt for screen, television, radio, records, have uniformly resulted in cuteness, bad acting, sentimentality, unbelievability, and hogwash.* Even Mark Twain himself got so fussed up writing it that at one point he calls Becky Thatcher Bessie Thatcher.

Nobody can even touch that book or even stand near it without doing something wrong. Even the *book is wrong*.

How can the book be wrong? The Master wrote it that way. That must be the way he wanted it. Not necessarily. He wrote by the automatic writing system, intuition, not from his brain. He had no powers of critical self examination and didn't really know how he was doing. He had terrible writer's blocks during the writing of this particular book and he kept freezing up and abandoning it. It took him eight years (1876–1884) of intermittent hacking to finish it, during which period he finished seven other books. He obviously had trouble with the much-discussed disintegrating last half which barely holds together and is heavily larded with nonsense, and when he was finished he had no idea what he had on his hands. But he liked it. Earlier, when he had written 400 pages he told Howells, "I like it only tolerably well, as far as I have got, and may possibly pigeonhole or burn the MS when it is done." Now he said "*I* shall *like* it, whether anybody else does or not."

But though it is probably "the greatest book ever written in America" it has many faults, and is very uneven and lumpy, largely because, as Bernard De Voto — Mark Twain scholar, Mark Twain psychiatrist, Mark Twain explainer,

---

* The only messing around with Mark Twain that ever came near catching the truth was Hal Holbrook's *Mark Twain Tonight*.

Mark Twain idolator, custodian of the Mark Twain papers in the Mark Twain estate — has said: "His boundless gusto expended itself equally on the true and the false."

Some of De Voto's remarks, in *Mark Twain's America*, are startling. I wonder if Hemingway and the rest of the "Huckleberry Finn Club" have ever pondered on these matters?

The opening is just *Tom Sawyer* and pretty poor *Tom Sawyer* at that.

Discussions of ransom and Tom's exposition of Aladdin's lamp are feeble.

After a first half . . . Mark's intuition begins to falter occasionally.

When the Duke has Louis XVII learn a Shakespearian speech compounded out of Sol Smith and George Ealer,* high and poetic reality lapses into farce. (Predictably. The necessity to carry a joke into cosmic reaches had betrayed him often enough before.)

Huck's discourse on the domestic manners of royalty is a blemish.

Huck's confusion . . . is perfunctory.

The concluding episodes of the attempted fraud . . . are weak in their technical devices.

The narrative runs downhill through a steadily growing incredibility.

* Sol Smith: early frontier humorist. George Ealer: Shakespeare-quoting pilot in *Life on the Mississippi*.

Mark was once more betrayed.

. . . a defacement of his purer work.

. . . incapable of sustained and disciplined imagination.

Well that's about enough of that kind of talk. Mark wouldn't have understood all this and his feelings would have been hurt. He not only wore his feelings on the outside of his skin but on the outside of his clothes.

In order to avoid a De Voto book-burning party at the library of your choice, let me add a few of his more characteristic pronouncements.

The book has the fecundity, the multiplicity of genius.

. . . as mature intelligence as fiction has anywhere.

. . . exquisite and delicate.

. . . the clearly seen individuals merge into something greater, a social whole, a civilization, seen just as clearly.

These scenes are warm with an originality and a gusto that exist nowhere else in American fiction.

No equal sensitiveness to American speech has ever been brought to fiction.

And much, much more. And De Voto concludes:

Whatever else this frontier humorist did, whatever he failed to do, this much he did. He wrote books that have in them something eternally true to the core of his nation's life. They are at the center; all other books whatsoever are farther away.

So good luck and mucho zdorovye to the Russians as they drift dreamily down the Dnieper and the second-unit director trips over Huckleberry and falls into the river. And we can't complain too much at them fooling around with our greatest American classic. After all, Hollywood made *War and Peace*, mostly by putting a pair of steel-rimmed spectacles on ole Hank Fonda and telling him to act like Pierre. ("You're this loser, see. . . . You tell him about it, Manny . . .")

> The director said he had been prepared to travel to Cuba in search of the right dark-skinned person to play the role of Jim, but accidentally came upon Mr. Immokuede at the university before undertaking the long talent-scouting voyage.

This points up what Fidel Castro has been saying all along. Only last week, while haranguing the cane cutters he repeated again: "Cuba not only invented baseball but has more black actors of the first class than any country in the world."

Rather a shame, in a way, that the director *did* discover that Nigerian geology student. If he hadn't, Judith Crist and Pauline Kael, not to mention Vincent ("Graffiti is Beautiful") Canby, would have been revealed before long anatomizing the immortal role of Nigger Jim as portrayed by a black Cuban speaking Missouri dialect in Russian with a Spanish accent.

> Mr. Daneliya wore a grey tweed jacket over a black turtleneck sweater as he discussed his film.

Having a turtleneck sweater is half the battle in artistic circles these days. So he's all ready to go and maybe he'll make it, especially since he's had the good sense to cast the part of the scrawny ole Duke with a Georgian named Vakhtang Kikabidze, "a singer with a Georgian band, 'Orera,' who speaks an accented Russian."

But I really don't have much hope for the project. It's dynamite. I don't care if Daneliya did also take his company to Lithuania "in the Baltic region, where he found places that to him evoked towns along the Mississippi." Such as Hannibal, Lithuania; Sainte Genevieve, Lithuania; East St. Louis, Lithuania . . .

Good intentions don't count. The material is precarious, holy, and producers, though beautiful human beings, are quixotic. The book switches constantly from hard reality to farce and burlesque, from naturalism to vaudeville turns. It is far too complicated for the constricted time allowances of the screen. Having said this, I suppose it will win an Oscar. So did Bondarchuk's *War and Peace*, which had nothing to do with Tolstoy, nothing to do with anything except the wonderful world of film entertainment, movie pages, movie grosses, cocktail chatter, reviewers' regurgitations, and Oscars. A movie is a movie but a Good Book comes Special Delivery from the angels.

But everybody wants to get into the act on Mark Twain. Papers, theses, and books on the subject continue to pour out of the brain mills. In the New York Public Library there are 12 inches of cards, packed tight, in the file drawer under "Clemens, Samuel Langhorne."

Scholarship on Mark Twain leads the literary trapeze artists to some conclusions that would have surprised Sam Clemens and given him more ammunition for his reiterated theory about the damn foolishness of the human race.

A soothsayer from the University of Texas proves to his own satisfaction that an incident in *Huckleberry Finn* is suspiciously similar in psychological construction to one in the *Uncle Remus* stories, *only in reverse*.

Representing Utah State University at Logan, another seer gives us: "Poe's 'The Cask of Amontillado': A Source for Twain's 'The Man That Corrupted Hadleyburg.' "

And Joseph Brogunier of the University of Maine has discovered a gossamer thread between the death of Myrtle Wilson in *The Great Gatsby* and the death of Boggs in *Huckleberry Finn*.

In *Tom Sawyer Abroad* Huck says "the darlingest place there is," and "there was a dear little temple." These unfortunate phrases are cited as evidence that Huckleberry anticipated "Juvenile Gay Lib" by nearly 100 years.

Such exercises are harmless and certainly as much fun as the evening crossword puzzle or "Dear Abby." It's when the heavy thinkers haul out their big guns that one seizes his coat and runs up the aisle and out to the Burger King.

In an attempt to "suggest rational alternatives to some current irrationalities in criticism and pedagogy," a modern scholar gives us this explanation of how Mark Twain happened to write *Huckleberry Finn:* "The motivating impulses behind the creation of a new fiction to study and express the nature of boyhood seem to have been blended of a sense of cultural discontinuity and a prescientific psychologism bred from realistic tendencies."

Thus speaketh Edwin H. Cady, Rudy Professor of English at Indiana U. in *The Light of Common Day; Realism in American Fiction.* The Professor now calls for the Disston and proceeds to saw the lady in half. It seems there are two conceptions which Mark Twain developed in the writing of *Huckleberry Finn* and *Tom Sawyer:* "One is a blend of conjectural history with Darwinism: that psychogenetically, ontogeny recapitulates phylogeny. . . . The other is a cognate, pre-Freudian psychology which conceives neither of psychodynamics nor of the search for identity."

Well, Professor Cady, thanks a lot. And it was real nice of you to take time off from your work to come and talk to us tonight and leave this message with us. Especially with the snow outside, poor trolley service, and all.

All I can think of is Sam, up at his desk in the billiard room in Hartford, chain smoking cigars, then pacing, going into the guest room and looking out the window down at the carriages and delivery wagons going up and down Farmington Avenue, waiting for the moment, for a scene, for a line of dialogue that would start the machinery, and then sitting down and writing, writing as only he knew how, oblivious to ontogeny.

Scholastic gymnastics involving *Huckleberry Finn* make humorous reading, of course, and they keep the Professors and the 11,000,000 Graduate Students in the land from wandering onto the field during football practice and getting crushed in the scrimmage. But so far they haven't really cleared up certain obvious peculiarities about the book which make me nervous and at times even as irritable as Mark Twain belaboring the memory of poor Charley Webster or spraying *The Leatherstocking Tales* with sulphuric acid.

So what are my complaints about *Huckleberry Finn?* The book is a National Shrine like Mount Vernon so it is pretty ticklish to start tormenting it. Obviously it is a real original and it was written by some kind of a genius and some kind of a nut. But I don't read it again and again as so many people claim they do. In fact I have read *Penrod* a good many more times. (Yes, *Penrod*, by Booth Tarkington, you heard me. As a matter of fact I believe I will read it again tonight.)

If I am bothered by anything in the book it is by the many factual impossibilities which none of the perfessors seem to notice.

Huck and Tom are pre-pubescent boys. They are twelve years old. Little guys in knee pants with squeaky voices. Kids this age are afraid of big guys, afraid of the town constable, afraid of the principal, afraid of strange dogs, afraid of bull snakes, afraid of bats and toads, afraid of their father's razor strap, afraid of the wind in the trees at night, afraid of owls, ghosts, and the dark. They also get sleepy by nine o'clock and are dead at nine-thirty.*

Yet here is the way Mark Twain makes them behave:

At *midnight* they crawl out the bedroom window into the pitch black, or spooky moonlight, and slide down drain spouts or over shed roofs to the ground. Six or seven of them meet, all having performed the downspout act, and they go down to the vast, fearsome Mississippi River associated chiefly in their minds with drownings.† They "unhitch a skiff" and all six or seven of them pile in and row down the river "two mile and a half" or 13,200 feet. Then they climb around in the night in the brush and woods until Tom finds the entrance to a *cave*.

You and I wouldn't go into that cave in the middle of the night for anything. Ernest Borgnine, Joe Namath, or even plucky little Truman Capote wouldn't go in that cave and

* Leslie Fiedler in his famous and fairly sensational essay on Huckleberry Finn points out that Huck's "praying for fish hooks indicated a mind at the five-year-old level."

† I was raised on "poor John Mehlhop," same age as Mycroft, who drowned in the Mississippi as a boy. Drownings were frequent and dwelt upon and called "drowndings."

neither would fearless John Glenn. But these little tads they light candles and "crawled in on our hands and knees." All six (or seven) of them are now crawling and holding candles at the same time, no mean feat, and they crawl *two hundred yards* which is six hundred feet, into a black hole full of bats and God knows what creepy things. The cave then opens up some and they get into a room "all damp and sweaty and cold." By now it is way past 1 AM and we find seven kids of pea-shooter age and some even younger, two and a half miles downriver from town and six hundred feet inside a damp cold cave. Then they have a *meeting*, if you can believe such a thing, and fool around in that cave talking an outlandish brand of cute "boy-talk" for about an hour. There is only one kid there with an atom of reality — Tommy Barnes.

"Little Tommy Barnes was asleep, now, and when they waked him up he was scared, and cried, and said he wanted to go home to his ma . . ."

But this puts Tommy at about the age of eight or nine. How in the hell did *he* get out of the house in the middle of the night? When is somebody in the graduate school at De Pauw University going to get worked up over *this* example of pre-Freudian omblongus?

They crawl out again, six hundred feet through clay, bugs, worms, bats, and they row *upstream* two and a half miles. The current of the Mississippi is about three miles an hour or more so it takes about two hours with that crowd aboard to row back up to town. Then they all split, climb *up* downspouts again, without disturbing a living soul, not even the kid brothers or big brothers they sleep in the same bed with. No. No brother wakes up and says "You dern fool where you ben all night? It's nigh onto sun-up."

Don't it just wipe the varnish off anything you ever heard of?

The puzzle here is that this fantasy was written by the same man who took a really mean attitude and a sadistic delight in exposing publicly the implausibilities of behavior in the works of James Fenimore Cooper. But *Huck Finn* is simply loaded to the guards with grotesqueries. De Voto and the others mostly pick at its vagaries from the point of view of style, balance, form, and artistic lapses.

Here are a few more mysteries.

Huck suffers from having to sleep in a bed at the Widow Douglas's so every once in a while he "used to slide out and sleep in the woods." Where and how in the woods? Just on the ground? Why would a kid do that? He wouldn't. Or has anyone ever suggested that perhaps Huck was a little bit "mental" as they say in Dubuque, meaning he hasn't got all his buttons. The Great Fiedler mentions that Mark Twain seems to insist that Huck is practically an animal, "a survivor from cave men."

Huck's escape from the cabin on the island is worthy of a full-size hero from Victor Hugo. Can't you just see a twelve-year-old kid planning that all out and then shooting a razor-back hog, dragging it into the cabin, and hacking its throat with an ax? Cut it out, Sam, will ya?

Just for fun, or for the meanness of it, I once made a time table of Huck and Jim's raft trip — number of days or weeks floating, number of villages worked by the King and the Duke, and the way I figured it, by the end of the trip they must have been about fifty miles beyond the Passes and out in the Gulf of Mexico.

I could go on and on, as Mother says when she is telling all the funny things that happened on her trip to Mineral

Point. But I will leave you go. If I was to get onto the famous Kemble illustrations, which at one point shrink Huck down to the size of Spanky McFarland, or the foolishness with pie plates, or the temperance joke, or Sarah Mary Williams and some trifles like that, why we would be here all night.

One could say of *Huckleberry Finn* what Huckleberry Finn said of *Tom Sawyer*. He said "That book was made by Mr. Mark Twain, and he told the truth, mainly. There was things which he stretched, but mainly he told the truth."

And speaking of *Tom Sawyer* . . . but don't let me get started on *that*.

And just to prove that all the bad news these days doesn't come from Washington D.C. listen to this:

Variety, December 6, 1972
A NATURAL SEQUEL
HUCKLEBERRY FINN

Filming of a musical adaptation of Mark Twain's *Huckleberry Finn* is going forward by United Artists and The Reader's Digest Films. . . . Film will be lensed on same locations as . . .

LEWIS MUMFORD TO VAN WYCK BROOKS

"Dear Van Wyck:
De Voto is, fundamentally, a jackass."

VAN WYCK BROOKS TO LEWIS MUMFORD

"Dear Lewis:
I agree that De Voto is an ass . . ."

Old Quarry
Guilford, Conn.
December 17, 1972

Richard Bissell, Esq.

Dear Sir:
In reply to your inquiry regarding the number of times *Huckleberry Finn* has been filmed, our files indicate the following:

1920: With Lewis Sargent.* Directed by William Desmond Taylor for Paramount. Silent.

* As to your question "Who is Lewis Sargent anyway?" we are pleased to report that 5 months after *Huckleberry Finn* he hit it big again with *The Soul of Youth*. That was in 1920. His next (and last to date) film seems to have been *The New Adventures of Tarzan* in 1935. So, if he is not a very good actor, he sure is some hibernator!

1931:   With Junior Durkin. (Although playing the title role Durkin was billed under Jackie Coogan who repeated the role of Tom Sawyer he played in the film of that name in 1930.) Directed by Norman Taurog for Paramount. Sound.

1939:   With Mickey Rooney. Directed by Richard Thorpe for MGM. Sound.

1960:   (*The Adventures of*). With Eddie Hodges. Directed by Michael Curtiz for Samuel Goldwyn Jr. (MGM release) Sound/color.

Finally, you asked if Wesley Barry played Huck "in a later version." Our records do not indicate that he did. However Mr. Barry did star in a silent version of *Penrod* and it is possible that you are confusing these two not dissimilar parts. This is a trick of the mind increasingly associated with advancing age.

Sincerely,

SPENCER M. BERGER

(Mr. Berger is a founder and the first president of the Yale Film Associates, adviser to the Yale University Film Collection, and a film collector and historian.)

SEVENTEEN

Say It Again, Livy
A PLAYLET IN TWO SCENES

Dramatis Personae

PAPA, later on, YOUTH
SUSY, a pretty, precocious child of ten, daughter to PAPA
LIVY, wife to YOUTH, mother of SUSY. A fragile, sensitive
woman of ethereal beauty who has had her sensibilities
pretty well bludgeoned by YOUTH, who while very tal-
ented is something of an oaf.

Scene I

Hartford, Connecticut. The third-floor billiard room of a
mansion, also used as a study by PAPA. The time is a snowy
winter afternoon in the year 1883. Snow is seen falling outside the windows.

PAPA is discovered smoking a cigar and writing at his
desk, Right.

PAPA (*Writing furiously*)

If they don't like it they can lump it. There! (*Picks up his writing and scans it.*) Pure gold!

(*Enter* SUSY)

SUSY

Excuse me Papa but could you come down to the school room? We're putting on such a lovely play. And it's very dramatic.

PAPA

Oh Susy, I can't. Don't bother Papa now, my dear. Papa is busy writing a classic.

SUSY

Oh Papa, not more *Huckleberry Finn?* You know Mama will ex-purgate it some more. Why don't you write another book full of lovely charming ideas like *The Prince and the Pauper?* You know perfectly well it is unquestionably the best book you have written. Oh Papa it is *perfect*.

PAPA

Don't worry dear, this one will pin their ears back or I miss my guess. It's my first classic, you know.

SUSY

But Papa, *Tom Sawyer* is awfully good, too. Don't you think it might be a classic some day?

PAPA

Not on your Paige tintype setter my dear Susy. That's just a children's book. Why it's so farfetched it makes me blush. So run along dear, and have a nice time. Writing a classic is no laughing matter.

(SUSY *crosses to door Left.*)

PAPA

By the way dear, did you hear Mama talking to Cook? Is anyone coming to dinner?

SUSY

Yes, a few. Let's see. Mr. and Mrs. Thomas Bailey Aldrich, and Mr. and Mrs. General Grant, and Joel Chandler Harris, and Mr. Howells, and Mr. Thomas Nast, and Mr. Andrew Carnegie, and Mr. Charles Warren Stoddard, and Mr. Bayard Taylor, and Mr. Bret Harte . . .

PAPA

What, that scoundrel Harte here again! Probably wants to touch me for a hundred. He already owes me three hundred and fifty good iron men. Why that despicable sponge . . .

SUSY

. . . and the Reverend Twitchell, and Mrs. Stowe, and Mr. Henry Rogers vice president of Standard Oil, and the Baroness Alexandra von Gripenberg, and Mr. Louis Tiffany, and Mr. Dan de Quille, and Mr. Holmes, and Mr. Longfellow, and Mr. Emerson, and the mayor, and the governor, and . . .

(*Exit* SUSY.)

PAPA

There you go. That's the trouble with being the most famous person in America, England, France, Germany, Asia, and the Hottentot Islands. Well, I'll clown it up for them, they expect it, wear my white cowskin slippers, act outrageous, they love it, reel off the *Golden Arm* and get rid of them early. Hope Carnegie brings me a few boxes of good cigars. All he sent me last week was a barrel of whiskey from his private distillery in Scotland. Where was I? Oh yes, Boggs says "I'm on the waw-path, and the price uv coffins is a gwyne to raise." Beautiful stuff, beautiful. (*He resumes writing.*)

(*Curtain*)

Scene II

The bedroom. PAPA is ensconced in an ornate, heavily carved double bed. He is smoking a cigar and reading his manuscript. LIVY in dressing gown or "wrapper" is brushing her hair before a mirror. The time is after the party, one AM. Outside, the snow is still falling, in large fluffy Nineteenth-Century flakes.

LIVY

Oh Youth, Youth, must you smoke those vile stogies in bed?

YOUTH
(*formerly* PAPA)

Dad blame it to tarnation. Consarn it and gol ding it all to a crosseyed mud turtle and a crippled hearse horse, I'm a son of misery and . . .

LIVY

Youth, Youth, I can't endure this obscenity. What's gotten into you lately? I declare, you're as gruffy as an old bear.

YOUTH

You'd be owly too, my dear, if you were writing a classic. Makes me nervous as an Arkansas schoolmarm with a garter snake in her bustle. First classic I ever wrote. Knocking out all that pot-boiling stuff like *Innocents Abroad* and that damn frog story is one thing. But this time it's a ring-tailed rouser and no mistake. I guess *this* will button up Holmes, Lowell, Longfellow, and that Boston bunch. But writing a classic from which all modern literature will come is no child's play, let me tell you. Why, it's as bad as piloting the *Grand Republic* through those bluff reefs at Xerxes Island on a pitch black . . .

LIVY

Yes, yes, dear. We know all about that.
(*Aside*) We ought to, we've heard it nearly as much as "the damned human race" around here, Lord knows.
(*To* YOUTH) Now just try to calm down my dear. All that champagne, and hot toddys and brandy isn't good for you.

Of course we're proud that you're writing a classic that will express the ferment and ineluctable force of the ever river-borne juvenescent democracy — a tale which will, with its superb patterns of speech from the raw frontier and its ruthless delineation of passionate affirmations of midcontinent fecundity, multiplicity, teleology, provocation, addition, subtraction, long division, not to mention intuitive cognition, intellectual virtuosity, and bumbosity, piston poppet valves, immortal prose, heroic concepts, superhuman imagination, deft touches, roaring wit, soaring genius . . .

YOUTH

Wait a minute, Livy! Say that again, that last part.

LIVY

Heroic concepts, deft touches . . .

YOUTH

No, no, not that, the last part!

LIVY

Soaring genius?

YOUTH

Now you're on your marks! Drive her, Livy! Come full ahead, girl! Say it again, Livy.

LIVY

Soaring genius, Youth! Soaring genius!
  (YOUTH *lights a fresh cigar.*)

(*Slow curtain*)

EIGHTEEN

A Steady Diet

Well here's another "springboard," as Freddie Brisson, producer and husband to Roz Russell, used to say to me when we were working on a script. Freddie and Roz were international celebs but unable to qualify for the Jet Set because Roz refused to fly.

This "springboard" comes from *Image*, the WNET Channel 13 program guide which I receive because I am a very heavy benefactor, to the tune of 15 dollars a year. In discussing a film that he made, based on the life of Swedish dramatist August Strindberg, producer Jack Kuney says of his meeting with the star, Max von Sydow:

When I first met von Sydow, I was already deep under the hide of August Strindberg, the strange playwright whose life I was about to film. As Max and I talked, I couldn't resist showing off my newly acquired knowledge of this giant of Swedish literature. The facts that I had assembled were not surprising to the actor, for every Swedish schoolboy grows up knowing Strindberg, *the way we in America thrive on a diet of Mark Twain.*

Those are my own private italics.

This springboard catapults me right on top of the idea that this notion is a large ring of Trenkle's baloney sausage. It's the kind of a cliché like the one about every good American constantly gorging himself on apple pie. Why, none of the restaurants that editors take me to in N.Y. even have apple pie on the menu. Next: All American boys hate school, play hookey, and "go fishin.'" I have raised three sons and none of them knows how to bait a hook and now they are big grown men: one's a lawyer, one's a banker, and one is a shill with a travelling carnival.

Let's assume "everybody" has at least read *Tom Sawyer* and *Huckleberry Finn*. Have they? Not by a long shot. Not many people who I met on the river had read either one, or *Life on the Mississippi* either. Oh that's not fair! *They* don't read anything! Oh yes they do, they read all the time. But they're not on a diet of Mark Twain. And neither is anybody else.

Lately at parties I've been wearing a trench coat and a snap brim hat and casing people's libraries while they were passing around the celery stuffed with roquefort dressing and the petrified Cheesy Snax. Listen Ace, you wanna know something? These people are on a diet of John Updike, Jacqueline Susann, Solzhenitsyn, Peter De Vries, David Halberstam, and Gardening Books. Some of them have a book called *My Favorite Things* by Dorothy Rogers and *all* of them have a big fat book by William L. Shirer. If there's any Mark Twain around it's a copy of *Tom* or a copy of *Huck* in the kids' room, most likely abridged ("adapted for younger readers") and with cute color illustrations. (In the Harper kids' edition the illustration of Tom and Becky lost in the cave reveals Tom as about eight years old and Becky stretching seven. This book has a gold seal on the dust jacket that says it has been "tested.")

I picked up a prep school catalogue the other day — let's just say it's the biggest and richest prep school in New England. I presume that the younger stewed cats read *Huckleberry Finn* and parts of *Life on the Mississippi*. Maybe they read the "Jumping Frog" for socio-historical reasons. This school is so advanced now that they have seminars in special subjects. In the English department these include seminars in Black Literature (yawn), an "extensive and intensive" seminar on William Faulkner, and — hold it — "The Fitzgeralds, a study of Scott and Zelda, their relationship and their works." There are also seminars on Irish literature, Russian literature, Shakespeare, and "the short story since J. D. Salinger."* But no Mark Twain.

What would a "diet of Mark Twain" be like?

MARK TWAIN DIET
(*Drink lots of water*)

	Calories
MONDAY	
Breakfast: "Captain Stormfield's Visit to Heaven"	3
Lunch: "Personal Habits of the Siamese Twins"	1
Dinner: The Gilded Age	8
TUESDAY	
Breakfast: "What is Man?"	3
Lunch: "The Double Barrelled Detective Story"	2
Dinner: A Tramp Abroad	12

* Who is "J. D. Salinger?" Is he the one that wrote "Mile a Minute Romeo" in *Western Story* mag?

WEDNESDAY
Breakfast: "John Chinaman in New York"   1½
Lunch: "The 1000 Pound Bank Note"   3
Dinner: Pudd'nhead Wilson   16

THURSDAY
Breakfast: "Journalism in Tennessee"   0
Lunch: "The Man that Corrupted Hadleyburg"   4
Dinner: Following the Equator   11

FRIDAY
Breakfast: "How the Author Was Sold in Newark"   ½
Lunch: "1601"   2
Dinner: Tom Sawyer Detective   3

SATURDAY
Breakfast: "The Undertaker's Chat"   1
Lunch: "Those Amazing Twins"   2½
Dinner: The American Claimant   7

SUNDAY
Breakfast: "Adam's Diary"   1
Dinner: The Mysterious Stranger   3
                        and
        Joan of Arc (with caper sauce)   0
Tea: Tom Sawyer Abroad   3
Late Supper: Letters from the Earth   1½

These items, all of which would of necessity appear on a "steady diet of Mark Twain" have for the most part gone stale with age and are totally inedible except to starving scholars in garrets, and they cause instant heartburn. The present-day scourges of American living such as "wetness," "five o'clock headache," "Why Are Your Sheets Whiter than

Mine?" and juvenile caries would, if this diet were followed, be eclipsed by a new and highly profitable national calamity called "Clemens stummick." In other words, nationwide dyspepsia on a scale never dreamed of by those who live by catering to the sloppy construction of the human body. Little old ladies from Fort Dodge holding thirty-five shares of Tums, Rolaids, or Pepto-Bismol would soon be seen by the pool at the Fountainbloo with their hair dyed blue. At the Brown Palace and in the Connaught Grill people would point and say, "Why shouldn't he have the five most beautiful women in America living with him? He got in on the ground floor with Gelusil, Maalox and Cow Brand baking soda."

So let's try not go to overboard. Suppose we keep in mind the celebrated quip: "Everybody talks about Mark Twain but nobody seems to know just exactly what-all he wrote."

As a matter of fact just the other day I was talking to a Swedish schoolboy who was appearing at Lincoln Center in an international, multilingual spelling bee.

"Listen Lars-Eric," I asked him backstage. "Do you eat much Strindberg at school?"

"I suppose you mean Stinky Strindberg in the sixth grade," he replied. "If that big clown gets fresh with my girl friend Helga one more time I'm going to let him have it."

NINETEEN

A Ride and a Treatment
at the Same Time

B art Molo soaked me $800 for the *Floating Cave*. It was probably, at that time, which was 1948, worth about $100, if he could have found a buyer, but except for me there was nobody in the whole wide world that craved companionship with that old shanty boat. Actually he didn't want much to sell it, it was hauled out high and dry down there at the Molo Sand and Gravel Yard in the harbor and they might need it again some time for the dredge crew, you could never tell. But I was back home again from steamboating, living up on the hill and raising a family, and I had sold my big beautiful houseboat *Prairie Belle* to the Grant Construction Company during the war. (They took it over to the Illinois River on a job where a deckhand kicked over a kerosene lantern like Mrs. O'Leary's cow and that was the end of the *Prairie Belle*.) I couldn't live uptown and keep my health and good spirits without a houseboat to retire to from time to time and there it was, sitting there month after month out of the water.

So I persuaded Mr. Molo to sell it to me. This isn't the best way to get a good price on something, especially from Bart L. Molo. So he socked it to me and I was all smiles and gratitude. That's the way I am when I get an obsession about acquisition and Mother says I will end up in the poor house. The only boat I ever paid the right price for was when I bought a 50 cent raffle ticket down in Maine and won a brand new Nova Scotia dory. It is well worth 50 cents and is different from any other boat I ever owned by being *new*. As I gaze back downstream at the river of my life I see a long procession of other people's boats that I have made my own: some of them sinking, some of them with stuck valves, soft planks, fritzed water pumps, Goldberg steering rigs, clanking rods, obscene paint jobs — and I loved them all. (Mycroft violated this rule and he went over to Chicago and bought a *new* Chris Craft runabout. This boat is now 25 years old but since he bought it *new* and nobody else ever owned it, it is still a *new boat*. He has never had the cylinder head off this engine — *new boat*, you see — in 25 years and it cruises at a steady 38 m.p.h.)

This houseboat that I extorted from Bart Molo was a two-room deal on a wooden barge built around the time that Farragut and Porter were bombarding Vicksburg. The first thing to do was launch it. So for no extra charge Molo's sternwheel steamer *Harriet* put a line on her and hauled her down the ways into the water.

Fully aware of who the new owner was, a longtime loser in the world of boats, she sank. She sank until there was two or three inches of water in the house and remained thus. I knew in advance that the seams were dry but not *that* dry. Once again — in the matter of marine property at least — I had revealed that "instinct for failure" which W. D. Howells ascribed to himself and Mark Twain. Everybody in the harbor enjoyed my discomfiture, not to mention vexation, since there is nothing that makes people so happy as to see some poor son of a bitch in trouble. When Tom Roshek sank his big houseboat *The Ark* in Dubuque harbor a few years later he provided more joy than the fall festival.

My pride of possession was in no way diminished. I don't mind too much if a boat is sunk as long as it's still *mine*.

I talked to Danny about it. I said I had a notion to let the Boat and Boiler pump her out and fix her.

"Listen Rich," he said. "Don't do that. Did you ever look real close at them shipyard owners' eyes? They have these little dollar signs in them."

So I hauled it out *myself* and fixed it *myself*. Mycroft came down to look it over and he said it was a fair successor to that weird old newlyweds' apartment of ours called The Cave, so he named it the *Floating Cave*, which it has been ever since. And it is still going, 25 years later, and it has seen a lot.

It was a funny houseboat and kept getting funnier all the time over the years. Danny and I knocked out one end and made it entirely glass with some old windows from when they tore down the A. A. Cooper mansion on 5th and Bluff Street. Then Danny built some bunks and he painted the kitchen pink because we had two gallons of pink paint he found on the town dump. Next he spliced an outhouse on one end which stuck out over the water into space. This curious jakes had two doors on it. You could enter from one deck and exit to the other deck. Don't know why this struck people as funny. But it did. We had a wood range in the kitchen and one wall was papered with pages out of a 1913 Sears Roebuck catalogue, the ladies' underwear and corset section. We put curtains at the windows and got some furniture in there and had a nice little home.

In winter we kept the *Floating Cave* in the harbor. Danny got married and spent his honeymoon on it with the temperature twenty below outside and not much better inside.

In summer we kept it on the Mississippi down on the island above Shinkles Bar, across from Nine Mile Island. Tied up just inside the point of the island, we could see all the towboats go by right close up. We had a camp ground, a big tree house, a garden, and a big bull snake. The house was empty all week, the doors were never locked but what you could get in with a jackknife or a claw hammer but in those times we never lost a thing.

At about this time I bought two sets of big Navy signal flags off that bargain page in the Sunday New York *Times*. That's the main reason we went to the trouble of ordering the Sunday *Times* — all those surplus bargains in tropical hammocks, size 13 boots, 15-gallon Army stew pots and such things. For a lark we hitched the signal flags together and hoisted them up between two tall elm trees and we left them up there all weekend. They looked "real purty."

This is another story about the anemia of the human brain machinery.

On Monday in the midst of an argument at the factory about the Reece buttonhole machine I got a phone call.

"Do you have a place on an island down the river?"

"Yes I do."

"Were you flying signal flags on Saturday and Sunday?"

"Yes I was."

"Would you mind telling me who you were signaling to?"

"Wait a minute, who are you?"

"This is the Federal Bureau of Investigation. We've had a complaint."

"What kind of a complaint?"

"We've had a complaint that you are signaling to flying saucers."

I have told you this story exactly as it happened.

After a few years the hull of the boat gave out so we filled it full of oil drums. When those rusted through Duncan Glab had two pontoons made at Morrison Bros. and we shoved them underneath. In the course of time the whole underpinnings as well as the pontoons said they had made their peace and were ready to go and they called for the priest. That winter Danny built a whole new barrel rack on the ice next to the old *Floating Cave*. Then he got a crosscut saw and sawed the house into pieces and moved it in hunks over onto the new hull and put it together again. When the ice went out, the new hull began to droop at both ends so Danny put hog chains on it. Johnny Bissell painted an impressive mural on the outside of the overhanging WC. Passing fishermen admired this and also the large replica of the Mona Lisa from Neisners dime store art department nailed to the exterior of the house up forward. The fishermen also slow-belled past to study and speculate on the eighteen-foot dugout canoe which I bought in Ecuador, hanging in slings under the eaves. (The only person in the family who could paddle this sensitive vessel without instantly tipping upside down with head stuck in the mud was my thirteen-year-old daughter Anastasia.)

During all these jocund and sometimes delirious years on the river at Dubuque there was a constantly changing roster of towboats and power boats. They all had strikingly exclusive characteristics, like dogs, and are remembered with affection. None of them survive except Mycroft's *Diamond Jo*, his wife Susie's super deluxe speedy flatboat *Nick*, and the mighty diesel towboat *Canton*.

The Original NICK: Twenty-four foot Mississippi type flatboat with 25 hp. Gray engine giving top speed of 12 m.p.h. Built in 1934 by Nick Balatz, a Bohemian fisherman.

Nick was not from Greenwich Village he was from Bohemia in the Old Country. He and his wife Mary lived on an island below Spechts Ferry. He was a fisherman and had his own pound. When the new dams flooded him out he went to farming in Wisconsin but he was never the same again away from the water and went into Slow Slump. The remains of *Nick I* are under a tree out on the farm at Mother's place. It is all bones, like the boat that the archaeologists dug out of the clay in the Thames estuary last year.

The CORK: My first rowboat after getting married and "settling down." ("I hope now that he's married Richard will settle down.") This boat was light as a cork when bailed out. But it spent most of its marine existence tied to a stump and filled with water up to the oarlocks.

The MORTAR BOX: My second rowboat. Named by Mycroft, for obvious reasons.

The GREEN HORNET: My third rowboat. Paul Adams and Eddie Chalmers borrowed this boat from me in the fall of 1949 to go duck hunting down at Green Island and I haven't seen it since. Listen, you guys, how would you like it if somebody borrowed your boat and never brought it back for 24 years?

The LUNCH: One day in 1965 I went to lunch at the Page Hotel in Dubuque with Mycroft and Susie. After lunch we went down to wander around in the new Sears Roebuck store down by the Maizewood plant.

"Why don't you buy a boat, R.P.," Mycroft said. "You haven't bought a boat in over a week."

"It won't cost as much," I said, "as if we had had lunch at

Sardi's," so I bought a 10-foot flat-bottom aluminum rowboat.

Mycroft calls this handy craft the *Lunch* but my children, of which I have four, call it the *Out to Lunch*.

The STEAM HEAT III: Smallest boat in the fleet being 8 feet long with a 3 horse Champion power plant. Nephew Freddie used this boat for prolonged and extensive bouts of cheerying.

The CITY OF CASSVILLE: My first power boat — a lightweight shingle of a boat made by Jack Erie of Cassville, Wisconsin, out of redwood. Power house featured 85 horse V-8 Ford conversion which made this craft get up and fly. No reverse gear. Tendency toward extreme cavitation in choppy water. Used as family boat for several years at which point without any warning it fell apart off Royal Arch Daymark and we all had to swim home.

The DEANNE: Garage-built cabin runabout constructed of Douglas fir plywood and sporting a Dodge conversion equal to 80 horses. At top speed this boat pushed tons of water ahead of it achieving, rarely, a speed of perhaps 13 m.p.h. I bought this boat because I wanted the boathouse it was in and the owner wouldn't sell the one without the other. This was during my effulgent period when I was attempting to corner the market on all the power boats on the Upper Mississippi. The *Deanne* was a slow coach and steered badly.

The TREATMENT: Danny Fetgatter's 18 foot flatboat with 1 cylinder Scheppele engine giving a top speed of 6 m.p.h. When under way this boat shook like an Aspen tree. Tom Roshek used to say "That's some boat Danny has got now.

You get a ride and a treatment at the same time." The inside of the *Treatment* was grey with age and weather, and every plank and frame was saturated with machine oil and patinated with fish blood and scales. The 1 cylinder engine having been started by snapping the flywheel, the "treatment" would begin; and the operator, quivering with St. Vitus' dance, would navigate with one hand, and, as various aged seams opened with the general palpitation of the hull, he would be seen wielding the bailing scoop more or less continuously.

The FOIL: Danny got himself a welding outfit and built him a boat out of steel. Mycroft and I went down to see how he was coming along with it. To save on the expense he was using a very light grade of steel plates. Leave it to Mycroft, a couple of days later he said to me, "How's Danny coming with the *Foil?*"

The BUREAU: Steel hull launch-workboat which I bought at auction from the U.S. Army Corps of Engineers at Le Claire, Iowa. Twenty-eight feet long, with a Kermath engine throwing a big wheel. I sank this boat in the Clinton pool in a storm, along with Danny and my nephew Johnny Bissell. It is still on the bottom, but they are O.K. It was used for work on the old Hennepin Canal and was named for the town of Bureau, Illinois, not for a chest of drawers. One of my favorite boats.

The SPITT: Danny's combination towboat, houseboat, cocktail lounge, ice breaker, and shop. Hard to classify. It was nearly as broad and as tall as it was long and looked like a 1920's tourist cabin with a pilot house on top going down the river. Enormous Gray marine engine providing a speed of 3 m.p.h. A very outstanding contribution to local marine architecture.

The BECKY THATCHER II: Paul Adams's sternwheel pleasure boat. To describe all the mechanical features of this boat would require a degree from M.I.T. and I haven't got one.

The CANTON: Thirty-four foot all steel towboat bought at auction from U.S. Army Corps of Engineers at Rock Island, Illinois. Built at Rock Island by C.O.E. in 1928. Powered by 114 hp. Buda 691 diesel engine. This boat was originally 28 feet long but was stretched and present engine placed in 1942. The *Canton* is a pushin fool. I'll tell you one thing I have had more fun with this boat than dear old Ari has had with his god damn yacht. Boating fun, that is. There ain't enough room on the *Canton* for that other kind of fun as it is mostly engine and deck; and the girls don't go so much for those diesel fumes but they are like Chanel No. 6 to me.

This exemplary workboat has nothing Chinese about it and was named for the port of Canton, Missouri, on the Mississippi River.

And that's not all. There was the *Alert* and the *Clytie* and the *Vidie;* the *General Plankton* and the steam launch *Ruth* and the awe-inspiring *Eldorna;* the *Dizzy Bee* the *Four Biller* and the *Lola* and the *Extravagance*. The National Marine Museum on the Thames at Greenwich will never see their equal.

Well now for some griping.

There aren't any funny boats like these around any more that I can see. I went up the river from Dubuque to Minneapolis last year, 275 miles, and all I saw was tin boats from

Sears Roebuck with eggbeaters hung over the end, modern streamline self propelled "houseboats" that look like house trailers caught on a flood, and plastic cruisers. Nobody seems to build boats out of their imagination any more and nobody tinkers with engines; they call for the mechanic who arrives in a white suit like a doctor.

There is now a "marina" every few hundred yards on the Upper Mississippi and I think I will go into the business and here's how to do it:

Get two big cottonwood logs and nail some rotten boards across for the float, leaving a few nails sticking up in various places. Con some gas company into the gasoline end of the deal including a great big sign. Now get yourself a second-hand soft drink machine that is out of order but don't put any Out of Order sign on it, and jimmy it so it will take and keep the coins but deliver no pop. Throw around about 300 empty quart oil cans, rusty gas cans, a busted washing machine, lots of empty beer cans and pop bottles, etc. A kiddy's tricycle with one wheel missing is not a bad idea. When all is ready, go to Albert Lea, Minnesota, to visit your wife's folks but leave the key to the gas pump and the oil shed with Bud Moody who tends bar at the Pastime Tavern. Leave a sign on gas pump that says "Open. Get Key at Pastime."

If you haven't got folks in Albert Lea go on up to Waukon, Iowa, where they are opening a new filling station and you get "a free chicken with each 10 gallons of gas."

After I moved away to gorge on the great immovable cultural feast of the Northeast coast I kept the *Floating Cave* across the river in South East Dubuque in a river slough called Frentress Lake. On one occasion beavers built a house completely around one end and underneath. When I went out last spring several mallard ducks were lounging on the deck. They didn't like the look of things and after talking it over among themselves decided to waddle across the deck and fall in the river. Some bad boys had broken a window so the ducks could get in and I found six duck eggs under the icebox.

Finally the oil drums went the way of all pressed steel and fell into decline. Lyle Bonnet hauled the old girl out one more time, put in some new timbers and inserted large bats of Economy Size New Miracle Styrofoam. So there she sits in Frentress Lake, brooding on the past, standing sturdy and staunch and very frowsy; and wondering, like the little toy dog, when those kids are coming back, and all the funny ladies and gentlemen with booze glasses in their hands talking and talking and talking and falling in the river. And when is that little girl going to come back and paddle around in that dugout canoe?

Floating Cave, dear, that little girl is now a big girl and lives on West End Avenue in New York City with a view of the Hudson River and she has tickets to the ballet and she shops at Bonwit's and discusses Bertolucci at tea in the Palm Court and has dinner at Bo-Bo's.

But the *Cave* figures she will be back some day. Uncle Mycroft is taking care of her dugout canoe. Who knows?

And sometimes, I feel sure, as she checks into the Land of Nod in her genuine Higgins brass bed after a glittering evening in tinsel town she murmurs "Oh *Floating Cave*, old houseboat, I will return."

TWENTY

And the Girls Are Waving at Us from Opekiska

Sometimes a youngster comes along nowadays and says to me, "Captain, do you think I could learn the river?" and I like to lean on an old pilotwheel and say, "Well, son, it's hard to tell about that. Some of the big, husky fellows I've taken on to 'learn' weren't any account at it — wasted four years — all for nothing. Then again, some little puny fellow who didn't look as if he could whip a cat, just up and comes in a winner. One thing certain: you can't *make* a pilot out of *anybody;* a man has to have it born in him; pilotin' comes natural."

CAPTAIN FREDERICK WAY, JR.

The other day I got a letter from a friend of mine who I used to deck for when he was mate of the big old Federal Barge Lines sternwheel steamer *James W. Good*. He went on up the ladder while I was going down it, riverwise, and has been a first class pilot for over thirty years. He is fearless, intrepid, and knows his trade.

Have been running from Beaumont, Texas, to St. Paul until this trip. We are making the first trip out of the new Mobil Oil refinery at Smith Hi Bridge below Joliet to East St. Louis.

Four loads, 10,000 tons and the river is high. Just finished

the Peoria and Pekin bridges and my blood pressure is get-
ting back to normal.

If he's so hot how come he worries about a little thing like taking 10,000 tons down through the Peoria and Pekin bridges "and the river is high"? Well he did it and now that it's over he feels good. He's beat the bridges again and his blood pressure is going down and he's satisfied. He knows how to do it.

"Ah, landsman, landsman — you can make nothing of this," says Charles Edward Russell, "it will be all alien and comical to you. But, landsman, you never steered a steamboat — you don't know, you haven't a guess! Even if your life has been crowded with triumph and brightened with good fortune, it is but a barren waste, never having known this."

A deckhand from Arkansas tells it a different way: "It's just like home in here on this boat. It ain't hard like in them cotton fields. I don't aim never to get off the river. Cap lets me hold her sometimes. He says some day I might just likely go for pilot."

And here's another riverman, reminiscing from the other world — for he has just drowned, at Lost Channel, above Lansing on the Upper Mississippi:

Funny the way I was standin there that day down by the river at Quincy and along comes old Buddy Hamilton but of course I never knew him then and he says to me "Boy," he says "how would you like to go steamboatin?" "Well Mister," I says to him like that, "I never did give it no thought. The fact is it never done entered my mind." That was the old *Western Belle* and it proves somethin how anybody could take to the river on that old deelapidation but I sure did and I never went back. Hand steerin of course and I'm in the pilot house whittlin wedges to make the windows stop rattlin and Cap Winans he says to me "Jacob, you see that big dead tree down there. Now here take aholt of the wheel and hold her on that tree while I go take a leak." Well that was just about it. Only two days before that I had ben stretchin bob wire and shovelin cow shit back on the farm and here I was steerin a steamboat down the Mississippi River. Well now I says this is somethin like it. The next day we come down through Chain of Rocks and past Burlington Elevator and on down through Merchants Bridge and McKinley Bridge and then down under Eads Bridge and I seen the lights of St. Louis and the boats tied up, the Federal boats and the Streckfus boats and the old *Ralph Hicks* laying idle and run-down and the show-boat and the *Golden Eagle* and the *Suzie Hazard* and them big smokestacks up in the air acrost the river at Cahokia and that was all I needed. She's been rough, tough, and brother Arthur got the farm and I got nothin. But if the true facts was to be made known, *he* got nothin and I got it all, because *he* was just a god damn farmer and *I* was a Mississippi River pilot.

You might say I laid it on pretty heavy when I wrote that, twenty years ago, but you are wrong. I know many and many old boys on the river that say it just the same way only different words. Like me myself up the Monongahela:

The twinkling lights of the town are beautiful and you're a hero. A pilot! What you dreamed of as a kid. The river is dark and mysterious, but it's your baby, you know it like a poem. You're the big cheese, it's all up to you. It's a real pilot house, real coal barges, and you're The Man.

Why don't plumbers, who now make no house calls and charge $47.50 an hour, exult in their craft like this? And carpenters, those envied members of the new elite who command the respect of both bankers and Cadillac-Oldsmobile dealers, do they rush out in the middle of the night to nail down birch flooring for the glory of it — do they discuss their mitre boxes with each other and say: "Thirty years with a Yankee drill in my hand and that's the toughest kitchen cabinet I ever installed. My nerves are shot! But I stand proud, I am a king among men, I stand apart, romance clings to me and my calling like number one grade clear pine sawdust, I've achieved the supreme ambition of every boy and man. And when I enter the bar of the Planters' House in my silk hat and apron full of finishing nails, a hush falls as captains of commerce, world famous phrenologists, and wealthy manufacturers of patent glue make way for me and timidly wait on my opinions. A murmur runs through the crowd: 'He's uncanny, he's a lightning whiz with dormers, drop siding, and porch railings. He reads blueprints blindfolded and can fabricate a gazebo in the dark. He ain't no man, he's a superman, he's a master carpenter!!' "

When I had put in my time and begged enough letters of recommendation from different pilots, I again presented myself and my credentials to the Inspectors at Dubuque. Captain Moffett and Captain Jones were mighty glad to see me and as before they rigged the bilge pump and pumped out everything that had happened to me since last time until the strainers began to suck and they figured they had it all and turned her off. After a rundown on local affairs, weddings, funerals, and harbor scandals, I settled down to write my examination for pilot's license and draw my map.

One part of the license for pilot is written questions about the Pilot Rules and whether you should blow for a dredge pontoon line across the channel and get them to open it or just bust your way through — things like that.

The other part is drawing a map of the section of the river over which you want to hold license. In order to do this you have to have been paying some attention to the river. You don't just draw a squiggly line and mark some towns on it — you draw a large scale detail map or chart of every mile. By large scale I mean about an inch to a mile. That means that if you want license from Minneapolis to the mouth of the Ohio at Cairo for example, your map will be about 856 inches long on something like 65 sheets of paper. If you want license to New Orleans just add 975 inches more onto this chart you have to draw out of your head.

On this map you must plainly indicate:

The channel
Islands and chutes
Wing dams (millions)
Buoys (hundreds)
All channel lights (hundreds)
Known bars, shoals, rock piles, or other features of the kind
Locks and dams with dimensions in feet
Cable crossings
Docks, landings, pilings, moorings
All bridges with span clearances in feet, and distances of fixed
    bridges above high water in feet

I can't keep up with the bridge builders any more but in 1941 there were twelve bridges between Minneapolis and the Belt Line Railroad bridge at St. Paul Park, a matter of only 17 miles. For your information the Robert Street bridge is 158 feet wide between sheer fences and the height is 62.6 feet above normal pool. How would you like to clog your head with this kind of information about every bridge on the Mississippi River, the Ohio, the Missouri, the Muskingum, the Sacramento, the Stikine, the Yukon, etc., etc., it's enough to drive a fellow mad I tell you. Help! Get me out of here!

Now about them wing dams, I am not going to get out my

chart and start counting, instead I am going to quote again the dean of Upper Mississippi River steamboating, George Byron Merrick. In 1909 he wrote: "There are less crossings now, but more dams and dikes — two hundred and fifty-one dams, dikes, and pieces of dikes in the little stretch of river between St. Paul and Prescott, a matter of thirty-six miles."

And there are twenty-nine wing dams between Dubuque Harbor and Shinkles Bar, and Ding Chamberlain, at one time or another, must of hit every one of them with his speedboat. On the other hand my brother Mycroft never hits anything. Some people are born that way. He can roar up from Nine Mile Island on a rising stage of water with the river full of drift on a pitch black night and never hit a thing. But if he says to me "Here, R.P., take it for a minute will you?" I am on top of an invisible saw log or a submerged oil drum within 30 seconds. That's just what happens to me in one of those damn speedboats at night. As a pilot I never hit nothing nor ever had an accident. But I am an expert at sinking small boats and putting them on the rocks. When we would be coming up some slough in a flatboat and somebody would say, "I wonder if that old wing dam is still in here someplace or if it is washed out?" Mycroft would say "Let R.P. steer. He'll find it. He'll hit it and then we'll know where it is."

That's what he calls me, "R.P.," because my middle initial is *P* for "Pike," like my famed kinsman Lieutenant Zebulon Pike who came up the river in 1805 and 1806 on his muchly overhuzzed expedition to the "Headwaters of the Mississippi River, through Louisiana Territory," a tour which bored my luxury-loving, civilized, irascible, ambitious cousin almost to death. His expedition illustrates perfectly "the creation of an artificial hero out of poor material," for when it was over he had "neither found the source of the river nor gathered any scientific or geographic information of value. His maps of the country were inaccurate and poorly drawn, his journal a jumble of contradictions and gaps. The Indian tribes who had accepted Pike's presents or listened to his long-winded speeches nearly all fought for the English in the War of 1812."*

Zebulon Pike had a brilliant career as a professional soldier, becoming a brigadier general at the startling age of only thirty-four, for which he is completely unknown. His career as an explorer was a complete barf, but for this he is enshrined for all time as a national hero.

Pike's outing was significant in that it marked the first appearance of the United States Army on the river in the role of an all-wise, stubborn old mother hen. And ever since that time the United States Army has held the firm belief that the Mississippi River belongs to the United States Army. In fact I had a bill from the Department of the Army in 1966 for tying up my houseboat to one of "their" islands. (Island No. 230, at Mile 574.5, if you must know.) They wanted 35 bucks. But they didn't get it.

So that's why my brother calls me "R.P."

I wrote and drew maps for four or five days and Captain Moffett said it was all O.K. and he had me raise my right hand and he swore me into the fraternity and pronounced me and the Mississippi River man and wife. So the first thing to do was to go over to East Dubuque and celebrate and get drunk, which is against the Pilot Rules but only if you are on a boat and performing wonders under your license.

Samuel Clemens and I both got our pilot's licenses in the month of April. I was thirty years old, he was twenty-four. Mine is dated at Dubuque, Iowa, April 28, 1943. His is dated at St. Louis, Missouri, April 9, 1859. Mine was for a

* Timothy Severin, *Explorers of the Mississippi*.

period of five years but his was for only one year. His license was issued under the Steamboat Inspection Act of 1852. Previous to that time there was no examination or licensing of pilots or engineers on inland waters. But the sound effects of steamboats exploding, colliding with each other, rending themselves on reefs and snags, finally got on people's nerves and the press and public made alarmed outcries. Congressmen and senators, fearing they might be thrown out and have to go back to work at the feed store, quickly passed the new bill.

Mark Twain's skill, or lack of it, as a pilot on the Mississippi, and his entire relationship to the river, has caused more wind than the 1871 cyclone at Coal Creek, Illinois, which blew the cabin and pilot house clear off of the steamer *E. Myron Grunt* and the pilot's gold watch 12 miles upstream to Rock Island, where it went through the roof and lit right on Fred Kahlke's desk undamaged.

Mark Twain himself created a big low-pressure area by his various highly romanticized and emotional statements on the subject, and by his omissions of truth. I think the truth — and getting at The Truth on Mark Twain is at least twice as difficult as Was Hamlet Really Whacky? — is that he was a good pilot but he didn't really like the fact as well as the notion, because piloting made him fidgety, that's what I think. If you have been reading this book and not just turning the pages while watching "Guiding Light" on the tube, you will remember my flood trip up the Ohio River. I was nervous, the captain was nervous, the only person aboard who was too dumb to be nervous was a deckhand from Scotts Run, West Virginia. So every pilot has plenty of times when he would rather be someplace else. But it seems Mark Twain was riding on his nerves most of the time.

And as for his running away from home to become a pilot

and achieve his boyhood dream, that's a lot of bug juice. It all happened by chance.

But what of his great and enduring love for the life of a pilot and for the river? Well, he quit. And he never went back for 21 years and when he did, in 1882, it was to take a ride the full length of the river, which bored the suspenders off him. And his visit to Hannibal nearly finished him off with bitter nostalgia and the curse of growing old. "I hate the past," he told W. D. Howells, "it's so damn humiliating."

Sam Clemens fell into steamboating and piloting quite by chance, despite what he said in later years. He saw a means of acquiring wealth beyond any uneducated young hick's dreams, plus prestige and adulation, which he craved and sought for all his life with an embarrassing childishness.* He did not run away from home, as he said he did, declaring that he would never come back until he "was a pilot and could come again in glory." He didn't run away from home at all, but Tom Sawyer would have said it that way so he said it that way and after he had said it a few times he began to believe it. Actually he was on his way to Brazil. Not Brazil, Indiana, but Brazil, Brazil, and the Amazon River where he planned to make another one of his fortunes, this time in "coca." He *happened* to take the steamboat *Paul Jones* at Cincinnati. Horace Bixby happened to be the pilot. When the boat reached New Orleans Sam happened to be broke. Brazil was O-U-T. He found that he liked it in the pilot house, he liked the river well enough, pilots were kings and they made 300 dollars a month. He decided to become a cub pilot. Then he became a pilot. When the war came and steamboating slacked off and pilots were no longer royalty and wages went down, he quit. He never went back or ever

* Van Wyck Brooks, Albert Bigelow Paine, and Mark's wife Livy all pinned "Arrested Adolescent" on his coattail.

dreamed of going back. All his talk about going back was sentimental guff, like that of the steel baron in his 65 room mansion who says he was happier when he was a puddler in the mill or whatever it is you do in a steel mill that makes everybody so happy to be there instead of in a 65 room mansion. Mark hauled this ballad out and played it on his banjo at frequent intervals — in 1865, in 1882, and he told Howells in 1874 that he would "quit authorizing in a minute to go piloting . . ." But he didn't. Closer to his real feelings was what he wrote to his sister Pamela in 1864, three years after he had just plain quit: "What in thunder are pilot's wages to me? . . . I have never *once* thought of returning home to go on the river again, and I never expect to do any more piloting at any price."

Some people say that Samuel Clemens' piloting was a nightmare to him and that he never drew an easy breath while at the wheel, and that he stuck it out for three years by sheer pluck. They say that the last time he rang off the engines and walked out of the pilot house was the biggest relief to his nervous system of his entire life.

First, what kind of a pilot was he? Despite the assertions of levee loungers, short-order cooks, wire-rope salesmen, Guggenheimers, omniscient bartenders, English teachers, licensed refrigeration engineers, and other authorities who say Mark Twain was a lousy pilot, the fact is that he was nothing of the sort. Over a period of four years he was regular pilot on about ten steamboats operating in the tricky-treacherous trade between St. Louis and New Orleans. One of his boats was the *City of Memphis*. He wrote to his fuzzy, John-a-dreams brother Orion that "it is the largest boat in the trade and the hardest to pilot, and consequently I can get a reputation on her."

All right — now according to his chief, Captain Horace

Bixby, "Sam Clemens never had an accident either as a steersman or as a pilot, except once when he got aground for a few hours in the bagasse (sugar cane) smoke, with no damage to anybody."

So he was a safe pilot, and careful, and conscientious. But that's not the whole story. In 1912, after Sam was dead and Bixby felt he could speak freely, Bixby had a few other things to say. With the bluntness and emancipation of old age, and perhaps with a good bit of cantankerousness born of his being asked foolish questions about Mark Twain over a period of forty years — ("Captain Bixby, what does it feel like to have been Mark Twain's boss on the river?") — he finally let the cat out of the bag, inside which it had been spitting and clawing since 1858 or thereabouts.

In a private, not-for-publication interview with Joe Curtis, river editor of the Memphis *Commercial Appeal*, the illustrious Captain Horace Bixby said: "Sam never was a good pilot. He knew the river like a book, but he lacked confidence. This developed in him soon after he came on my boat. It never left him. . . . Sam Clemens knew the river, but being a coward, he was a failure as a pilot."

There's nothing so mean as an ornery old man. Sam wasn't a failure as a pilot, because he was constantly employed, never was fired that we know of, and never had an accident. He wasn't a "coward" or he couldn't have even backed one of those elegant monsters away from the landing by himself much less stand watch after watch. What he was, and I have seen it on the river, was a *nervous pilot* — uneasy, apprehensive, fidgety, high-strung. In the not-so-new idiom of our times I think it is safe to say that bearing the sole responsibility for an enormous steamboat and the lives of its passengers gave Mark Twain a flaming case of "anxiety neurosis."

I don't claim originality for this idea.

"It is not without interest," Delancey Ferguson wrote in 1943, while I was in the steamboat office drawing my maps, "to speculate how long Sam would have lasted on the river without a nervous breakdown had he continued to be a pilot."

That's a stiff drink, but two things seem to bear it out.

The first is that he never, ever, had anything to say about his life *as a licensed pilot*. Never. No time, no way, not a word. He dug a hole someplace and buried these years, and scattered leaves and trash over the grave and never went back.

The second is that he had The Dream.

Mycroft and I have The Dream but we have it about final exams at college: We've just discovered we have to take the final examination in a subject we didn't even know we were enrolled in. The exam is crucial and there's no way to prepare for it; the exam is in an hour. Hopelessness and fear are the general themes and it is not enjoyable.

"Had The Dream lately?" Mycroft says to me when I haven't seen him for a while.

"Yeah," I say. "Last month."

"So did I," he says. "What was yours this time?"

" 'Europe since 1815,' for Christ sake."

The human brain is a strange contraption. Mycroft graduated from college 42 years ago, I graduated 37 years ago.

Mark Twain had The Dream. It was about the river, about piloting. And about hopelessness and fear. It's a bad one. In a rare moment of candor, not knowing what he was spilling, I'm sure, he told his biographer, Albert Bigelow Paine, the following, in the year 1906:

There is never a month that passes that I do not dream of being in reduced circumstances, and obliged to go back to the river to earn a living. It is never a pleasant dream, either. I love to think about those days, but there is always something sickening about the thought that I have been obliged to go back to them; and usually in my dream I am just about to start into a black shadow without being able to tell if it is Selma Bluff, or Hat Island, or only a black wall of night.

I hope and pray to the Superintendent of Dreams that when Sam slipped away into eternity at Stormfield in 1910 he was not facing that black wall of night, wanting to set up a jingle jangle in the engine room and stop her, back her away from disaster, but paralyzed, unable to reach for the bell cord. I hope instead he was back at the house on Farmington Avenue with Livy and the girls and the girls are opening their Christmas presents and it is snowing outside and Joe Twitchell and the Warners are coming to dinner and there is no damn steamboating, no damn Horace Bixby, and no damn Mississippi River.

He deserved it. I wonder if he got it?

I have plenty of dreams about steamboating days on the river but they are all happy dreams and I don't want them to end. But I was a deckhand and mate a lot more than I was a pilot so when I go trucking back to the barge line via Dreamland Express I am most usually on deck, working with the boys and the barges and having a good time, and young again, and it's like Joseph Conrad says: "Wasn't that the best time, that time when we were young at sea; young and had nothing, except hard knocks — and sometimes a chance to feel your strength . . ."

Why did *I* go on the river? Did I run away from home vowing never to return until I could come back as a pilot "in glory"? Not likely. Dubuque doesn't associate glory with being a towboat mate or a towboat pilot or a towboat anything. If I had gone to Florida and come back as a trick water skiing champ *that* would have been glory in Dubuque. And after I became the toast of Broadway and spent all my evenings drinking Rheingold beer out of the wardrobe mistress's Enna Jettick shoes that was glory on Main Street. But not the barge line.

I went on the river because I liked boats all my life and I liked the river and I had already been a deckhand on the river and the deep sea and I liked the smell of engine rooms and I loved those big steel barges and I liked river people and I liked the talk. I liked to wear a black cap with a shiny visor and swell around a bit and talk about "When Cap knocked down the Hastings bridge," and "The last time we were in drydock in St. Louis," and I liked to cuss the company and hang around in saloons with other rivermen and our girls and act tough. I actually liked to go ashore in the yawl with the mate and flounder around in the brush and the mud in the middle of the night getting a line onto a cottonwood tree. I liked to feel that I was romantic, hard boiled, hard working, and a hard case.

I was also of draft age, and as I said before, there was a great big war on, and I didn't then and don't now want any part of the United States Army.

I enjoyed the work, I wallowed in the life of the rivers. It made my whole life then and since worthwhile.

And, *we were moving the coal.* We were taking 10,000 tons out of Alton, Illinois, and shoving it up to Genoa, Wisconsin, and to Winona, Lake City, Red Wing, and St. Paul, and to the Republic Coal Co. in Minneapolis, right below the Falls of St. Anthony, and directly to the University of Minnesota Coal Dock in order to feed the boilers and keep the professors and the pink-cheeked coeds warm and happy through those long sub-arctic winters.

Down on the Tennessee we were moving that grain upstream and taking that pig iron down. Keeping things moving for Walt Whitman, John Dos Passos, Thomas Jefferson, Henry Clay Frick, Knute Rockne, Lewis and Clark, Lou Gehrig, Carl Sandburg and Tom Mix.

From the Lower Mississippi we were pushing and sweating that fuel oil north against the brutal current and thence into the Ohio for the homes, stores, factories, saloons, bawdy houses, schools, hospitals, and morale-building pool parlors of Cincinnati.

On the Illinois we bunted the coal from Havana into wild Chicago for the lovable Commonwealth Edison Co., to keep the mazdas burning all night and to light up those cat's feet in the fog.

Way over on the Monongahela with our miserable little stink-pot pushers and our beat-up, senile standard barges we were feeding thousands of tons of coal to the mighty Du Pont plant where it was converted into high explosives to rain wretchedness and calamity and second thoughts on the Hun.

Transportation is not only an adventure, it is a satisfaction to its perpetrators. This satisfaction is evident in a steamboat cook but it does not apply to barge-line presidents and members of the board. Their satisfaction lies in dictaphones and annual reports. The real satisfaction and the real power come from participating in the actual transport. When the big shots and the money changers used to come aboard for lunch on the old *Mackenzie* at Cincinnati in their iron suits it was obvious that we, not they, were the lords of the river and of all creation.

Every couple of weeks or so I, too, dream that I am back

on the river. Sometimes we've got barges loose all over the river, like down at Mark Twain light on the lower. Or we're coming down through Pine Bend below St. Paul on a beautiful fall day and Winslow is up in the pilot house and I'm out on the tow with the boys, rigging the pump for a leaker. And sometimes I'm in West Virginia piloting again and it's June and the girls in their summer dresses are waving at us from Opekiska and I give them a toot on the whistle and Curly Harden comes into the pilot house to relieve me and he says "Hey Beedle, how would you like some of that?" Anyway I have a grand time and when I wake up I am at home and the old lady is here and so is old dog Tray and that's the way I like it.

Everybody's life on the Mississippi is different. Sam had his and I had mine.

And I'm only a stranger here, and I ain't got no frog; but if I had a frog I'd bet.

APPENDIX

Study Helps

Questions on the text: 1. Tell in your own words where the Mississippi River is located at. 2. Do you think the Author knows what he is talking about? Why not? (Project: Make a simple model of your idea of the Author's brain.) 3. Outline the history of Oregon up to the time of the boundary treaty of 1846. 4. Draw a map showing clearly the location of Hannibal, Missouri; East Dubuque, Illinois; Harold's Club; Birthplace of Grover Cleveland Alexander.

Additional Readings

Mississippi River

Scheibert, Justus, *Das Zusammenwirken der Armee und Marine, Eine Studie illustriert durch den Kampf um den Mississippi. Mit zahlreichen Karten.* Rathenow, 1887.
An indispensable work.

Bishop, Nathaniel H., *Four Months in a Sneak Box. Boston*, 1879.
2,600 miles in a duck boat down the Ohio and Mississippi and along the Gulf of Mexico. Crazy.

Quick, Herbert, *Mississippi Steamboatin'*. New York, 1926.
Mr. Quick says to hear Mark Twain tell it there was nobody else on the crew of a steamboat except the pilots.

Blair, Walter, *A Raft Pilot's Log*. Cincinnati, 1929.
Blair was the last pilot to take a steamboat up Fever River to Galena. A very cantankerous old gent. My dear mother-in-law of Davenport,

Iowa, now deceased, as a girl was once allowed by Captain Blair to "hold the wheel" of the *Helen Blair* while under way below Le Claire.

Eads, James B., *Physics and Hydraulics of the Mississippi River*. New Orleans, 1876.
Not recommended for hammock reading.

Hennepin, Louis, *A New Discovery of a Vast Country in America*, etc. Chicago, 1903. (First pub. in French, 1697.)
Father Hennepin embroidered the truth to such an extent that he was known all over the territory as "Le Menteur."

U.S. Engineers Dept. *Report on Bridging the Mississippi* between St. Paul, Minn., and St. Louis, Mo. Washington, 1878.
Too bad fellows. Most of the damage had been done by 1878.

Shaw, Eugene Wesley, *The Mud Lumps at the Mouths of the Mississippi*. U.S. Geological Survey, Dec. 20, 1913.
All you've always wanted to know about this top-secret, sticky subject.

Spach, Louis Adolphe, *Les Antiquités de la Vallée du Mississippi*. Revue d'Alsace, Colmar, 1852.
Authoritative, but contains no reference to popular antiquities such as Captain Walter Hunter, Hattie Peaslee, or the pie at the old Illinois Central station lunch counter in Dubuque.

Long, Stephen H., *Voyage in a Six-oared Skiff to the Falls of St. Anthony in 1817*. Minnesota Historical Society, 1889–1890.
Shows what some people will go through to get their names in the paper.

Russell, Charles Edward, *A-rafting on the Mississippi*. New York, 1928.
May be the best book about the Upper Mississippi, at least in romance, nostalgia and throat-lumps, laughter through tears, poetic musings, dialogue and action.

Hilgard, Eugene W., "The Loess of the Mississippi Valley and the Aeolian Hypothesis." *Am. Jour. Sci.*, V 18, 1879.
A frank exposé of a subject usually discussed by pilots only in whispers.

Butler, Ellis Parker, *Swatty*.
A much neglected book. Kids in a rivertown (Muscatine, Iowa) in the early 1900's. (Butler wrote *Pigs Is Pigs*, a modern *Jumping Frog* which sold Millions.)

Houseboats and Houseboating

Beard, Daniel C., *The Jack of All Trades*. New York, 1900.
". . . idle people in England have introduced the HOUSEBOAT AS A FASHIONABLE FAD, which has spread to this country and the boys now have a new source of fun as a result of this English fad."

Adams, Joseph H., *Harper's Outdoor Book for Boys*. New York and London, 1907.
How to build a punt, a scow, a sharpy, a proa, a paddle-wheel punt, a side-wheel catamaran, a "house-punt," and a "house-raft."

Beard, Daniel C., *The American Boys' Handy Book*. New York, 1882–1910.
    "A Floating Camp, or the Boys' Own Flatboat." Plans for building a nice small houseboat. And Uncle Dan makes it just as much fun to read about as to build.

Speakman, Harold, *Mostly Mississippi*. New York, 1927.
    From the headwaters at Lake Itasca to Minneapolis by canoe; thence 1,828 miles to the gulf in a small houseboat. A "classic." The Speakmans stopped at Hannibal and interviewed Mrs. Laura Frazer, the original "Becky Thatcher," then nearly ninety years old. Since the old lady had been interviewed six or eight times a day for more than fifty years, she hadn't anything new to offer on the subject of Sam Clemens as real life prototype for the American "good bad-boy."

Mathews, John L., *The Log of the Easy Way*. Boston, 1911.
    Honeymooners drift for seven months down the Illinois and Michigan Canal, the Illinois River, and the Mississippi all the way to New Orleans. Real shantyboating, written in an exuberant style now passé.

Castlemon, Harry, *The Houseboat Boys*. Philadelphia, 1895.
    By the author of *Frank on a Gunboat, Frank on the Lower Mississippi, Frank Before Vicksburg*, etc. etc. Boys outwit crooks and thugs while floating down the Mississippi in a houseboat.

Bissell, Richard, *Good Bye Ava*. Boston and Toronto, 1960.
    Most of the action takes place on houseboats.
    "A boisterous fable . . ." Charles Poore, The New York *Times*.
    "Uproariously funny . . . the characters are racy . . ." Brooks Atkinson, the New York *Times*.
    "This book should be burned . . ." Scales Mound (Ill.) *Weekly Gazette*.
    "I wish Richard would get a steady job." The Author's Mother.

Winfield, Arthur M., *The Rover Boys on the River*. New York, 1905.
    Ninth volume in the *Rover Boys Series for Young Americans*. Further idiotic and unrealistic adventures of our friends Dick, Tom, and Sam as they bumble down the Ohio on the houseboat *Dora* with "eight sleeping rooms" plus "a bunk room below for the help." The Rover Boys are not so dumb and always have plenty of girls around, in this case Nellie and Dora. Perhaps a sample of this penuche will whet your appetite for more.

> "Help, help," added Dora. "Help us! This way!"
>
> "We are coming," came back in Dick's voice, and a moment later the steam tug crashed into the houseboat, and the Rovers and several others leaped on board.
>
> "Stand where you are, Lew Flapp," cried Tom, and rushed for the bully of Putnam Hall. "Stand, I say," and then he hit Flapp a stunning blow in the ear which bowled the rascal over and over . . .
>
> "Are you hurt?" asked Dick of the girls anxiously.
>
> "Not in the least, Dick," answered Dora. "But oh how thankful I am that you came as you did."
>
> "And I am thankful too," came from Nellie.

"And we are thankful to be on hand," said Tom.
And the others said the same.

Hope, Laura Lee, *The Bobbsey Twins on a Houseboat*. New York, 1915. "Rigorous . . . fruitful . . . solid . . . important . . ." *Commentary.*

Books Referred to in Text

Bissell, Richard, *A Stretch on the River*. Boston, Atlantic, 1950.

Brooks, Van Wyck, *The Ordeal of Mark Twain*. New York, Dutton, 1970.

Clemens, Clara, *My Father, Mark Twain*. New York, Harper, 1931.

De Voto, Bernard, *Mark Twain's America*. Boston, Houghton Mifflin, 1951.

Ferguson, Delancey, *Mark Twain: Man and Legend*. New York, Russell, 1943.

Howells, William Dean, *My Mark Twain*. New York, Harper, 1910.

Kaplan, Justin, *Mr. Clemens and Mark Twain*. New York, Simon and Schuster, 1966.

McLellan, Fraser C., *The Mon River and a Good Captain*. Privately printed. No date.

Merrick, George Byron, *Old Times on the Upper Mississippi*. Cleveland, Ohio, Arthur C. Clark, 1909.

Paine, Albert Bigelow, *Mark Twain, A Biography*. 3 vols. New York, Harper and Bros., 1912.

Thomas, Benjamin P., *Abraham Lincoln*. New York, Knopf, 1952.

Way, Capt. Frederick, Jr., *The Log of the Betsy Ann*. New York, McBride, 1933.

———, *Pilotin' Comes Natural*. New York, Farrar, 1943.

And as the Sun Sets over the Gas Works:

CARL BOWERS, 73, USES OARS TO GUIDE HIS HOME-MADE, 16-FOOT SKIFF HOUSEBOAT DOWNSTREAM IN THE MISSISSIPPI RIVER NEAR THE IOWA SHORE NORTH OF KEOKUK WEDNESDAY. BOWERS ACCOMPANIED BY HIS DOG, DIXIE, LEFT CAMANCHE NOV. 11 DESTINED FOR NEW ORLEANS

The Des Moines *Register*
November 23, 1972

So good luck to you Carl, and don't ram no bridge piers. And give them towboats plenty of room with their strings of barges or you and your dog Dixie might end up down below with the catfish. Remember, old timer, there is nothing, absolutely nothing half so much worth doing as messing around in boats — especially on the Mississippi River.